State Constitutional Conventions

From Independence
to the Completion of the Present Union
1776 – 1959

A Bibliography

compiled by
CYNTHIA E. BROWNE

introduction by
RICHARD H. LEACH
*Professor of Political Science,
Duke University*

GREENWOOD PRESS
Westport, Conn. ● London, England

Library of Congress Cataloging in Publication Data

Browne, Cynthia E
    State constitutional conventions from independence
to the completion of the present Union, 1776-1959.

    Bibliography: p.
    1. Constitutional conventions--United States--
States--Bibliography. 2. Constitutions, State--
United States--Bibliography. I. Title.
KF4501.B76   016.342'73'024   73-9327
ISBN 0-8371-7005-2

Library of Congress Catalog Card Number: 73-9327
ISBN: 0-8371-7005-2

First published in 1973

Greenwood Press,
a division of Williamhouse-Regency Inc.
51 Riverside Avenue, Westport, Connecticut 06880

Manufactured in the United States of America

Contents

Preface

The first thing users of this bibliography will want to know is what it contains, and secondly, they will want to know what it does *not* cover.

SCOPE

Basically, included here are all publications of state constitutional conventions, commissions, and legislative or executive committees, and all publications for or relating to these conventions and commissions issued by other agencies of state governments.

Naturally, the quantity and quality of available printed material vary widely from state to state. Later conventions were more loquacious than the comparatively taciturn earlier ones. The Thirteen Original States of the northeastern coast, on the whole, tended to publish more constitutional material than did southern or western states—and have had a longer period of years in which to do so. The British subjects who arrived on these shores in the seventeenth century were already politically oriented and articulate. Later settlers of the western frontier had too much else to think about at first to develop political sophistication. Some states have held conventions every few years to alter their constitutions or to frame new ones, choosing this process over other alternatives. Minnesota even staged two constitutional conventions simultaneously, one for Democrats and one for Republicans! Some states,

on the other hand, have retained their original constitutions, pre-
ferring to amend them periodically through the legislative process.
Since it is impossible to include every bill and legislative act for
amending a state constitution, a few representative examples have
been selected to demonstrate that this alternative constitutional
process is going on all the time between formal conventions. Sometimes, for lack of published records entire conventions, such as
Kentucky's of 1799 and Arkansas' of 1874, as well as all of
Georgia's earliest ones, were lost. Then the only recourse was to
depend on newspaper accounts, addresses to the people, copies of
the constitutions framed, and similar sources. Other conventions
published so much material that it was difficult to sift through the
mass for the most significant items.

A copy of each new or revised constitution, plus special annotated editions, are also included. The choice of editions was based
entirely on their official character and relevance rather than on
their antiquarian significance. Accuracy of text was the criterion
for selection, rather than first edition status or bibliographical
peculiarities that might render a document interesting to collectors.

FAILED
CONVENTIONS

Success and failure have been considered equally relevant to the
constitutional development of a state, and no convention has been
judged for inclusion on the basis of its outcome. Conventions
whose work has been rejected, either by the voters of their own
state or by the United States Congress, have nevertheless per-
formed a useful and interesting function, particularly as their rejected provisions sometimes turn up later in future constitutions.
New York is especially illustrative of this fluid principle. The constitution of New York's 1867-1868 convention was rejected by
the people except for its judiciary article, which became an amendment to the 1846 constitution. The New York Constitutional
Commission of 1890-1891 submitted its report too late for legislative consideration, but its proposals were adopted by the 1894
convention. The suggestions of the New York conventions of both

1915 and 1921 failed to win approval at the time, but many of their proposals were eventually adopted in 1925.

Some of the western states in particular experienced difficulties in entering the Union with their constitutions; the raw freedom of frontier society produced some rather radical constitutional provisions which were just a bit too democratic for the more conservative eastern taste. Fortunately, Wyoming's advanced notion about woman's suffrage seems not to have delayed statehood appreciatively, but Utah, which began holding constitutional conventions and petitioning Congress for admission to the Union even before the Civil War, tried again and again without success—until the Mormon Church finally disavowed polygamy in 1890.

Arizona's pragmatic approach to this problem of congressional approval is an interesting case in point. When its admission to the Union was vetoed by President Taft because of a clause in its constitution on judicial recall, the people of the territory removed the offending clause—just long enough to get through the formalities of admission—and then promptly restored it as soon as statehood had been achieved and Congress and the president no longer exercised control over the state's internal affairs.

Nevada, on the other hand, slipped easily, even illegally, into the Union, before it had even met the population requirement for statehood, because President Lincoln was so anxious for votes to ratify his Thirteenth Amendment to the federal Constitution. California's first constitutional convention was also basically illegal, having no authorization from the United States Congress or territorial assembly of any sort. It was proclaimed by the military commander of American forces, who assumed the role of *ex officio* governor under Mexican law, but public support was so strong that the constitution it framed was accepted and went into effect.

CONGRESSIONAL HEARINGS

An attempt has been made to stay on the state level and not get seriously involved in congressional hearings and presidential pro-

nouncements on state constitutional questions, but exceptions
have been made as required by historical significance. Kansas presented a special problem in this connection with its notorious Lecompton Constitution, which became a national issue instead of
remaining a local state one. This, of course, was because it involved the incendiary slavery question and thus sparked seemingly
endless congressional debate, with every state airing its official
opinion on the Kansas constitution on the floor of the United
States Congress. Had all of this voluminous material been included, the checklist would have been overweighted with viola-
tions of the announced intention of remaining on the state level
as far as possible. Therefore just enough details are included to
indicate the nature and extent of the national controversy en-
gendered by the Kansas state constitution and its unique role in
the subsequent election of Abraham Lincoln to the presidency.
President Buchanan's advocacy of the Lecompton Constitution
split the Democratic party and gave the Republicans a winning
campaign issue.

INDIVIDUAL
SPEECHES

It is assumed that speeches by individual delegates will be included
in the convention proceedings. Separately published speeches are
not listed, except in a few instances where special interest or significance seemed to justify inclusion—for example, those by William F. Switzler on the disfranchisement of Rebels in the Missouri
constitutional convention of 1865; by R. M. Cunningham on suffrage and elections in the Alabama constitutional convention of
1901; by the governor of New Jersey, Charles Edison, in 1943,
when the question of revising that state's constitution was pending;
and the speeches delivered at a dinner given in honor of Massachusetts Senator Daniel Webster by the Maryland constitutional convention in 1851.

NONOFFICIAL
PUBLICATIONS

Works about state constitutions and conventions which were not

issued officially by the conventions themselves or by agencies of
the state governments have not, as a rule, been considered for
inclusion. Since, however, the word "official" admits of a certain
flexibility in interpretation, a few borderline items have been
added. These include a draft of a constitution offered for consideration by a committee of citizens of Colorado in 1875, the
1924 Association for Constitutional Amendments of St. Louis,
Missouri, and a mock trial of one of the members of Pennsylvania's 1872-1873 convention, plus such unorthodox representatives as the 1914 conference on the question "Shall a Constitutional Convention be Called in Indiana?", the 1837 Convention of
Friends of Constitutional Reform in Utica, New York, and the
1910 Reunion of Survivors of the Constitutional Convention of
1890 in Jackson, Mississippi.

NONCONSTITUTIONAL CONVENTIONS

Experience in working with state constitutional conventions
demonstrates that the bibliographer should be wary of certain
years in convention chronology. Catalogers sometimes toss around
the adjective "constitutional" somewhat indiscriminately for state
conventions that convened to discuss national rather than state
issues. Between 1787 and 1790 state conventions usually met to
ratify the federal Constitution, and in 1933 they usually met to
ratify the Twenty-First Amendment to that Constitution, which
repealed "prohibition." These conventions are not within the
province of this bibliography. Yet it is unwise to take anything for
granted; in this connection, 1850, is a particularly tricky year for
the bibliographer. Some states held conventions in 1850 to consider the slavery issues involved in the controversial Compromise
of 1850, which admitted California as a free state, organized New
Mexico and Utah into territories without restriction, and abolished
the slave trade in the District of Columbia, among other provisions.
Michigan, on the other hand, actually did revise its own state constitution at its 1850 convention, and so did Maryland; these must
be included here.

TIME SPAN

The period covered by this bibliography is from the beginning of this country as an independent nation to the year 1959, when Alaska and Hawaii were admitted to the Union. This means that colonial charters or any other instrument of government in force prior to the achievement of American statehood—with the single exception of those for Connecticut and Rhode Island—are not included. Because of their uniquely independent status under the British colonial régime, these two states were able to transform their colonial charters into state constitutions by the simple expedient of removing the name of King Charles II from the texts. They continued operating under them until 1818 and 1842, respectively.

Likewise, this bibliography is not concerned with constitutional material relating to periods when certain states were independent republics, as were Vermont and Texas for a time. Vermont, which in 1791 was the first state to join the Union, continued to operate under the same constitution it had been using as an independent republic until 1793. Therefore Vermont's checklist starts with its constitution of 1785, but the legislative processes which brought it into being are not included. Unlike Vermont, Texas did not bring an earlier constitution with it into the Union, but instead held a convention to frame a new one before joining.

Excluding constitutions and the conventions or commissions which framed them in periods when the particular state was not a part of the Union raised the question of whether to include the secessionist conventions of 1861, since the southern states considered themselves to have withdrawn from the Union and to comprise a separate sovereign nation. The decision to include these conventions is based on the official United States government position that these seceding states did not possess the right or power to withdraw and therefore, logically, could never have left the Union. Thus the record of constitutional development in these states was not interrupted by eliminating conventions which were definitely constitutional in nature, if only to the extent of altering the

phrase in the constitution regarding the overall government to
which the state acknowledged allegiance. One of these conventions even spawned a new state—West Virginia—which grew out of
a Virginia convention on the excuse of disagreement over the
question of secession. Tennessee, like Virginia, was so deeply divided in its loyalties that it also nearly split in two, first voting
against secession and then, even after reversing itself in a second
referendum, continuing to have its eastern section represented in
the United States Congress by Andrew Johnson as late as 1862.
But the state remained intact after the war.

The decision to include the southern secessionist conventions on
the basis of their constitutional nature worked fine except for
Missouri, which held a secessionist convention, but did *not* secede.
The question then arose: was the Missouri constitution revised at
this time? Or, to put it another way, were the Missouri conventions
of 1861 to 1863 constitutional since the first one assembled to
vote on the question of secession and voted not to? The question
can be argued both ways. The decision in this bibliography in
favor of their constitutional nature is based on *Webster's Collegiate
Dictionary*'s definition of the word "constituent" as "having
power to form or revise a constitution." Subsequent sessions of
the Missouri Civil War convention assumed constituent powers,
deposed the pro-southern state administration of Governor
Claiborne Jackson, and set up a provisional government, headed
by Hamilton Gamble, with a rump legislature. The convention
did not revise the fundamental law of the state, but it did adopt
several constitutional amendments.

ARRANGEMENT

In general, the arrangement of titles within each state is chronolog-
ical by date of convention or constitution. Only Louisiana frus-
trates this plan for an outline of constitutional development.
For a few years the state operated under two constitutions at the
same time, the Supreme Court having invalidated certain provisions of the 1913 constitution, so that the 1898 constitutional
provisions relating to these particular subjects remained in effect.

North and South Dakota presented a special bibliographical problem from the point of view of arrangement because, although they were admitted to the Union on the same day as separate states, they had previously formed a single territorial unit. Cataloging has been solved by entering their pre-statehood conventions under the heading "Dakota Territory," but this solution is of no help in distributing titles between two separate checklists. In general, joint conventions have been assigned to South Dakota's checklist, as they tended to be held in towns situated within South Dakota's present boundaries, until 1889, when separate conventions were held, respectively, in Sioux Falls, South Dakota, and in Bismarck, North Dakota. Students of state constitutional development in this area would do well to consult the checklists of both Dakotas.

The gaps which occur in the code sequence of some of the states represent documents that could not be located, or items that duplicated material covered by another code.

SOURCES

The printed catalogs of the Library of Congress, the card catalogs of a number of large research libraries, and published bibliographies, both those of a general nature and those pertaining to individual states, have been consulted in compiling this bibliography. Special thanks are due to Miss Margaret Moody of the Harvard Law School Library, Miss Virginia Wood of the Yale Law School Library, and Mr. Albert Matkov, Massachusetts State Librarian, for their inestimable aid and cooperation. Space does not permit thanking individually the other librarians and curators all over the country who provided advice and material, giving so graciously of their time and labor. Without their help, this bibliography would not have been possible.

CYNTHIA E. BROWNE
Cambridge, Massachusetts
December 1972

Introduction

> State constitutional revision should have highest priority in re-
> structuring state governments to meet modern needs. Stress
> should be placed on repealing limitations that prevent construc-
> tive legislative and executive action, on clarifying the roles and
> relationships in the three branches of government, on permitting
> thorough modernization of local government in both rural and
> urban areas, and on eliminating matters more appropriate for
> legislative and executive action.
>
> **Committee for Economic Development**
> **MODERNIZING STATE GOVERNMENT**
> (New York: Committee for Economic
> Development, 1867), pp. 19-20.

Perhaps no other people is as attached to a written constitution as
the basis of group action as is the American people. In part, the
American devotion to constitutionalism can be said to be a natural
result of America's English heritage. By the beginning of the
seventeenth century, England had institutionalized her recognition
that some sort of balance was necessary between the power of the
king and the rights of the people. They were not very precise
about it, as was the wont of the English political tradition even
then, but there was general understanding that the power of government should be limited and that certain forms and procedures
should be acknowledged and followed by all who wielded political
authority.[1]

The British went on to utilize constitutionalism without ever developing a single written focal point within the system where its

meaning would be embodied, but they pointed their American relatives in a different direction by their practice of granting written charters to each American colony. Thus Americans from the first built on their English conceptual foundations a peculiar reliance on specific written authority to convert the concept into practice in the actual situation of colonial government. The Virginia Company of London, a joint-stock company, received the first charter for a settlement in the New World from King James I in 1606. That charter, Thomas A. Bailey has written, constitutes "a significant document in American history. It guarantees to the overseas settlers the same rights of Englishmen that they would have enjoyed if they had stayed at home." As other companies were formed (the Massachusetts Bay Company in 1629, for example) and other colonies were settled, the practice of chartering was extended and "soon became a foundation stone of American liberties."[2] As shown in Table 1, chartering did not always precede colonization, and not every colony received a charter, but as it turned out, they were merely the exceptions that proved the rule.

The colonial charters laid the basis for constitutional government in the New World. Not only did they speak to the rights of Englishmen, but they also provided for legislative assemblies and dealt to some extent with their powers and those of the Crown through the governor. They spoke to government matters only partially, however, and they were more often observed in the breach than otherwise. Even so, they aroused feelings of independence in colonial breasts and led Americans to confirm, out of their own experiences, the need for a written basis of self-government. The very fact that there were numerous recharterings in the 170 years of colonial history attests to their acceptance among colonial leaders.

Thus as independence came in 1776, and the Declaration of Independence converted thirteen independent colonies into thirteen independent states, one of the first tasks the new states felt to be necessary was the writing of state constitutions. In three colonies— Connecticut, Massachusetts, and Rhode Island—the colonial charter was considered sufficient, and it was reworded or revised so as to be appropriate for entities now sovereign in their own right.

TABLE 1
Charters Granted to the Thirteen American Colonies

Colony	Founder(s)	Date of Charter	Date of Founding	Status
VIRGINIA	London Co.	1606 (New charters were issued in 1609 and 1612)	1607	Royal
NEW HAMPSHIRE	John Mason and others	1679	1623	Royal
MASSACHUSETTS (Plymouth Colony, settled in 1620 by the Pilgrims, was unchartered; it merged with Mass. in 1691)	Puritans	1629	c1628	Royal
MARYLAND	Lord Baltimore	1632	1634	Proprietary
CONNECTICUT (New Haven, settled by Massachusetts emigrants in 1638, was unchartered; it merged with Conn. in 1662)	Emigrants from Massachusetts	1662	1635	Self-governing
RHODE ISLAND	Roger Williams	1644 and 1663	1636	Self-governing
NORTH CAROLINA	Emigrants from Virginia	1663	1653	Royal
NEW YORK	Duke of York (after the Dutch)	1664	1664	Royal
NEW JERSEY	Berkeley and Carteret	None	1664	Royal
SOUTH CAROLINA (The Carolinas were chartered as a single colony; they separated informally in 1691 and formally in 1712)	Eight nobles	1663	1670	Royal
PENNSYLVANIA	William Penn	1681	1681	Proprietary
DELAWARE	Sweden	None	1638	Proprietary
GEORGIA	Oglethorpe and others	1732	1732	Royal

Adapted from: Thomas A. Bailey, *The American Pageant*, 3d ed. (Boston: D. C. Heath, 1966), p. 17.

But in the other states, constitution-writing became the order of the day. Some of the states, indeed, were so confident of the outcome of the Second Continental Congress' proceedings that they began to work on their state constitutions in the spring of 1776. When the Second Continental Congress, on May 10, 1776—nearly two months before the Declaration of Independence was finally adopted—urged the colonies to provide themselves with constitutions as quickly as possible, the resolution was directed to the states that had not yet done so.

The colonial assemblies, now state legislatures faced with the responsibility for setting up the needed organic law, had few models to follow other than the colonial charters themselves. Thus those charters, in retrospect, were given even more significance. The first state constitutions were brief and limited in scope, providing little more than skeleton arrangements for state government. They were written in general language and tended to incorporate statements of general political principles. The authors of those first state constitutions were, after all, neophytes at providing democratic self-government (though it is now clear that such government had been practiced in the colonies to a remarkable degree), and they were forced to rely on broad concepts of, rather than on specific provisions for, the kind of government they knew they wanted.

Their experience carried them as far as the expression in abstract terms of the principle of separation of power within government; it did not carry them beyond to a working model of checks and balances. Indeed, the colonists tended to make the colonial governors and judges appointed by the Crown the villains of the time, and so they purposely limited executive and judicial power severely while putting their trust in the legislatures as representative of the people. They placed very few restrictions on the legislatures.

Attention was paid to qualifications for voting,and for office holding. But not much more was covered. A striking omission of some constitutions was an effective provision for amendment, and few included a rationalization of state power over local governments.

Colonial experience and conviction did suggest the necessity of *state* guarantees of rights (the national bill of rights, it will be recalled, was not included in the Constitution as the first ten amendments until 1791), so that the majority of the first constitutions also contained bills of rights. As might be expected, what emerged was a mixture of abstract principles and specific applications of some to issues arising out of the struggle against the Crown prior to the Revolution. There was considerable variation among the states in terms of the civil liberties guaranteed, and little was provided to convert statements of principle into actual fact.

Not surprisingly, most of the first state constitutions were hardly democratic documents. Requirements of property ownership greatly limited the exercise of suffrage, and some states even included religious qualifications for office. If these constitutions were cast in the name of the people, they did not conceive of the people in very inclusive terms, and as a rule they were promulgated and went into effect without direct popular approval.

But when it is recalled that all of the first state constitutions were drafted in haste, in response to a major emergency (revolution), one must conclude that they were admirable documents. Indeed, the longevity of some of the early constitutions (North Carolina's, for example, lasted from 1776 to 1868) attests to their basic solidity. In any event, it must be concluded that those early constitutions "were bold and audacious attempts to base government upon written documents which expressed man's rationality and belief in certain transcendant propositions."[3] If they did less well in providing for the later practice of self-government, it is because far less was expected of government as a whole in the 1770s and because our perception of the range of possibilities of free government developed only gradually, with experience.

There is no typical situation, unfortunately, which illustrates the general trends of subsequent state constitutional development. Experience with government in operation under the first constitutions revealed a number of defects, so that in most states either a number of amendments had to be made, if possible, or a new constitution had to be written before too many years elapsed. Most demanding of correction was the opening up of state gov-

ernment to representation of a larger proportion of the people.
Thomas Jefferson must be credited with inspiring a broad-gauged
movement to expand the base of political power in the United
States. The constitutions of all the states formed after 1787 were
written without reference to the property qualification for voting,
and the original thirteen states soon began to follow their example.
During the decade of the 1820s, the political role of the average
male citizen came to approximate in fact what the Jeffersonians
had long claimed for him in theory. By 1830, only Virginia and
North Carolina retained the freehold qualification and in due time
it was removed even in those states. *"Sovereignty of the people,*
the *equality of men,* and the *right of the majority,"* one of the
delegates of the Virginia constitutional convention of 1829 declared, had by then become the operating principles of American
state government.[4]

At the same time, beginning under Jefferson and flowering
under Andrew Jackson, a sense of the sufficiency of the individual
began to pervade American thinking and a concomitant requirement of *laissez faire* was thus felt necessary in state governments.
In an essay written in 1837, John L. O'Sullivan stated that no
government was to be trusted "with the power of legislation upon
the general interests of Society so as to operate directly or indi-
rectly on the industry and property of the community."[5] As far
as state constitutions were concerned, the impact of that growing
conviction, which lasted for more than a century and still is not
wholly gone from the American mind, was to open them to a
variety of restrictive amendments, made ostensibly in behalf of
the people. As a result state constitutions began to take on the
negative cast that marks them to this day.

Finally, it became obvious to others, as it did to Jefferson, that
under the early constitutions all governmental power in the states
had gravitated to the legislatures. "The concentration [of power]
in the same hands is precisely the definition of despotic government," Jefferson observed in his *Notes on Virginia.* "It will be no
alleviation that these powers will be exercised by a plurality of
hands, and not by a single one. One hundred and seventy-three
despots would surely be as oppressive as one. . . . An *elective*

despotism was not the government we fought for. . . ."[6] To reme-
dy the situation, both the constitutional position of the governor
and the power of state courts had to be strengthened, though to
this day the state governor is a pale shadow of the powerful
American president and judicial review is less meaningful in state
than in national courts.

In order to achieve these and other changes, the states came to
rely on two devices to bring about constitutional change—the state
constitutional convention and the amendment process. Constitutional amendment was and remains the most direct means of altering state constitutions. Not all the original constitutions, as has
been noted, provided for amendment, but by the early nineteenth
century, all state constitutions provided some way for their own
amendment. Ordinarily amendment involves legislative proposal
and ratification by the electorate, although in the West in particular, beginning in Oregon in 1902, some states also began to authorize amendments to be initiated by petition of a specified proportion of the voters. States vary considerably in their amendment
procedures, though there are two basic patterns: either amendment
provisions have been "so rigid . . . as practically to deprive the
people of the opportunity to alter their basic law, [or] so lax as to
encourage too frequent changes."[7] When the latter has been the
case, constitutions have come to resemble patchwork quilts, their
original material completely covered by amendments. Where the
former has been the case, the constitutions have ossified. Either
way, state constitutions became steadily more difficult to operate
under as the number of amendments increased, which it did in
nearly geometric proportions as the once simple constitutions became increasingly detailed and complex. The amendment process
is necessarily a limited one, however. By its very nature, it must
chiefly be confined to specific, partial changes rather than to
overall, architectonic changes. For that kind of change, the constitutional convention became, and has remained, the standard in-
stitution in American state government.

Massachusetts and New Hampshire were the first states to make
use of the convention device to write their original state constitutions. Indeed, the people of Massachusetts rejected the first con-

stitution proposed to them by the legislature, not only for what it contained but also because it had been prepared by the legislature itself instead of by a group of representatives specially chosen by the people. The legislature then ordered the election of a special constitutional convention, representative of the towns in the state and chosen by the electorate. That body met in September 1779, and the Massachusetts constitution of 1780 was its product. That constitution, much amended over the years, still serves as the fundamental law of the Bay State. The people of New Hampshire had the same conviction about distinguishing the mere legislative function of enacting statutory law from the constituent function of enacting organic law; therefore, they too insisted on a separate constitutional convention, which was duly convened in June 1779.

Thus these two states led the way in bridging the gap in the theory of popular sovereignty which the original state constitutions embodied. They believed the constitution-making power to be of such significance that it had to emanate from the people themselves. By devising the state constitutional convention, they provided the people with a way to convert their power into demonstrated fact. As the habit of using it developed, the nature of state constitutions themselves changed from something akin to ordinary legislation to emanations of the constituent power of the sovereign people, thereby confirming at the state level the arguments of the Federalists (and *The Federalist*) regarding the national constitution. Since those conventions, state constitutions have been regarded as a higher law to which all other acts of the people and its agents are necessarily subordinate. By the time Chief Justice John Marshall was to write his classic opinion in *Marbury* v. *Madison* (1803), it was generally accepted that state constitutions—created by the people and embodying principles the people believed to be fundamental and permanent—controlled legislative and executive acts repugnant to it. It was not much of a jump to carry the principle to the national level, which Marshall did in *Marbury* v. *Madison*.

Since those early days, there have been well over two hundred constitutional conventions in the states, convened to propose changes in the states' organic laws, in response to changes in the

body politic itself. As Albert Sturm sums it up, constitutional
change is demanded by the "changing political, economic, and
social conditions and problems of a growing nation." In the
United States, the major factors "contributing to constitutional
development include: population growth, expansion of popular
participation in public affairs through the extension of the suffrage, increase in the number of elective officers, and adoption
·in some states of the initiative and referendum; industrialization;
technological development, particularly in transportation and
communication; and consequent growth in magnitude and complexity of the functions and responsibilities of the state. Of
primary importance also is the change in the people's thinking on
the proper role of government in modern society. Formerly, it
was minimal; today extensive protective, regulatory, and service
activities reflect growing public desire for positive government."[8]
And of course the reapportionment revolution created by the Supreme Court's decisions in the 1960s has been a major contributing factor to constitutional change in recent years.
    The large number of constitutional conventions that have taken
place in America is not surprising. What may be surprising, however, is the states' acceptance through the years of state constitutions as political documents, which represent victories in the political process. "If politics 'is the study of influence and the in- ·
fluential,' as Harold Lasswell has said, and the 'influential are
those who get the most of what there is to get,' it is not too difficult to identify the 'influential' within a state by the privileges and
protection they have secured in their state constitutions."[9] Property groups—mining interests, cattlemen, cotton growers, pork
processors, furniture manufacturers, joined later by taxpayers
groups, veterans groups, religious groups—fought to secure privileges and exemptions (or to put it another way, to seal themselves off from the exertion of state power) in the fundamental
law of state after state, until constitutional conventions and the
amendment process came to seem more the tools of special groups
than of the sovereign people.
    Constitutional changes also came to be seen as "one of the
prizes in the power struggle between . . . political parties," which

serves to reinforce the volatile nature of the documents.[10] As
written, they were all too frequently the victims of "unclean
thinking and bungling workmanship."[11]

Because the struggle between groups for primacy in a democratic society is endless, constitution-tinkering became the leading
characteristic of American state government in the nineteenth
century. The story of New York's constitution is typical. The
state's first constitution was adopted at a convention in Kingston
in 1777 and was put into effect without submitting it to the
voters. It contained 6,600 words. It was replaced in 1821 by a
document containing 14,600 words and approved by the electorate. "Under the impulses of Jacksonian democracy, a new
Constitution, some 20,000 words long, was adopted in 1846."
It was amended a total of 23 times before it was replaced by New
York's present constitution in 1894. Counting 162 amendments
adopted in the intervening years, that document has some 47,000
words.[12] An attempt to rewrite that constitution in 1967 failed
at the polls in 1968. Constitutions in every state were amended
or partially revised endlessly, this detail and that provision altered
by one legislature and approved at one election, another part
changed by the next legislature and approved at the next election,
until most state constitutions have become so riddled with
amendments and revisions that they defy easy reading or understanding. As the process continued, constitutions often came to
have "superfluous, confusing, or even contradictory clauses."[13]
"To wade through the mass of conflicting and obsolete provisions,
in order to find the constitutional law on any point, was like
hunting for a needle in a haystack," Roger Sherman Hoar declared of the Massachusetts constitution in 1921, which was one
of the better ones.[14] Worse, as the Commission on Intergovernmental Relations concluded in 1955, "Many State constitutions
restrict the scope of effectiveness, and adaptability of State and
local action. These self-imposed constitutional limitations make
it difficult for many States to perform all of the services their
citizens require, and consequently have frequently been the under-
lying cause of state and municipal pleas for federal assistance."
Too often, instead of effectively providing "for vigorous and re-

sponsible government, [they] forbid it."[15]

For many years the constitutions of most states were altered so frequently that it was difficult to keep an up-to-date edition of them. The worst result of the process, of course, was that from their earlier place as the higher law of the states, constitutions slid down in precedence and priority to the level of ordinary law. They lost the special aura of sanctity that surrounds the United States Constitution, and came to be regarded as not much more than a set of statutes, to be altered or exchanged with each new majority in the electorate. A significant gap between theory and practice has thus opened up and it has yet to be closed.

It is precisely the evolution of this way of looking at state constitutions that has made state constitutional conventions, as well as the amendment process, central to an understanding of state government. Only through familiarity with the forces at work in each successive convention (or behind each move for amendment) can the central meaning of state constitutions in the life of an individual state be ascertained.

This phenomenon has not been confined to the state level of government in the United States. The national constitution, with its original generality preserved, has been kept alive by congressional action, executive and judicial interpretation, and custom and tradition rather than by revision of the document itself. Thus it retains both the theoretical and the actual flavor of fundamental law. But it is unique in this respect. Municipalities have compiled a record of dissatisfaction with their charters from the states, which has led to constant rechartering. And the thousands of constitutions of private organizations and groups are always undergoing change. The moral is clear: as soon as a constitution is made to serve more than basic purposes, it is pushed into the vortex of politics and there is no escape. Those purposes, Judge John J. Parker of the fourth U. S. Circuit Court once observed, "are twofold: (1) to protect the rights of the individual from encroachment by the State, and (2) to provide a framework of government for the State and its subdivisions." "It is not the function of a constitution," Judge Parker went on, "to deal with temporary conditions, but to lay down general principles of government which must be observed amidst changing conditions. [It is up] to the people's representatives to apply these principles through legislation to conditions as they arise."[16] Only when the people of the American states come to have the faith in legislatures that such a rule requires will it be possible for state constitutions to meet Judge Parker's specifications. That day is still far off.

Until then, American state government will have to continue to be based on imperfect foundations. Although no two state constitutions are alike, there is a basic similarity among them, and they cover much the same things in a fairly common pattern. They are for the most part old (see Table 2); they are prolix (some nearly the size of the Manhattan telephone directory!); they are heavily amended; and they are seldom logical in their construction. A typical state constitution might have fourteen articles, which, in approximately the following order, would cover:

Preamble

   1. Bill of Rights
   2. Suffrage and elections
   3. Separation of powers
   4. Legislative organization and procedure
   5. Executive offices and procedure
   6. Judicial organization, jurisdiction, procedure
   7. Military powers and state militia
   8. State finances and taxation
   9. Local government authorization and restrictions
  10. Public education
  11. Highways, public works, and public utilities
  12. Miscellaneous restrictions on legislative power
  13. Provisions re private enterprises—corporations, banks, railroads, monopolies, and trusts
  14. Amendment and revision procedures

Most constitutions are also characterized by considerable dispersion of material, a trait perhaps not easily visible in the above list; by the continued presence of nullified (by subsequent amend-

ment) and outdated (by the passage of time) provisions; and by
the use of archaic and hortatory language.

In recent years, there has been growing recognition that state
constitutions have departed too far from the ideal Judge Parker
described. Prodded by such works as former Governor Terry
Sanford's *Storm Over the States,*[17] by such reports as that by the
prestigious Committee for Economic Development on *Modernizing State Government,*[18] and by the efforts of such bodies as the
short-lived National Council for the Revision of State Constitutions, Inc., the postwar years have been marked by efforts to
achieve more workable state constitutions.

Indeed, constitutional reform probably reached its peak in the
late 1960s. In 1968-1969 alone, thirty-four states were reported
to be involved in "major surgery on their organic laws," while ten
other states had engaged in some type of constitutional revision
earlier in the decade. The current edition, 1972-1973, of the
Council of State Governments' *Book of the States* reports that
"approximately two-fifths of the States took some form of official action directed toward general constitutional revision during
1970-1971" alone. Three states—Illinois, Virginia, and North
Carolina—adopted new or extensively revised constitutions, while
three others—Arkansas, Idaho, and Oregon—rejected proposed
new documents.[19] "These summary figures reflect a continuing
high interest and concern among the States for modernizing their
basic laws."[20]

What is the thrust of modern constitutional revision? On the
one hand, as has been suggested, constitutional revision offers an
opportunity for a reshuffling of the dominant interests in a state
and for the claims of each newly victorious group to be reflected
in organic law. This political role, indeed, may be the chief use of
constitutional conventions.

But there is another thrust, and that is toward the improvement of the practice of state government. What would a "good"
state constitution be like?[21] Both scholars and practitioners have
come to agree on perhaps a half dozen characteristics of a sound
state constitution:

TABLE 2
General Information on State Constitutions

State or other jurisdiction	Number of constitutions	Dates of adoption	Effective date of present constitution	Estimated length (number of words)	Number of Amendments Proposed	Adopted
Alabama	6	1819; 1861; 1865; 1868; 1875, 1901	1901	106,000	474	320
Alaska	1	1956	1959	14,400	96(a)	7(b)
Arizona	1	1911	1912	16,000	132	69
Arkansas	5	1836; 1861; 1864; 1868; 1874	1874	40,170	(c)	53
California	2	1849; 1879	1879	68,000	646	375
Colorado	1	1876	1876	40,190	(c)	74
Connecticut	4	1818(d); 1965	1965	7,959	4	3(e)
Delaware	4	1776; 1792; 1831; 1897	1897	22,000	(c)	81
Florida	6	1839; 1861; 1865; 1868; 1885; 1968	1969	21,286	8	4
Georgia	8	1777; 1789; 1798; 1861; 1865; 1868; 1877; 1945	1945	500,000	921	691
Hawaii	1	1950	1959	11,882	35	32
Idaho	1	1889	1890	22,280	125	85
Illinois	4	1818; 1848; 1870; 1970	1971	17,500	0	0
Indiana	2	1816; 1851	1851	11,120	45	25
Iowa	2	1846; 1857	1857	11,200	38	33(f)
Kansas	1	1859	1861	14,500	86	58
Kentucky	4	1792; 1799; 1850; 1891	1891	21,500	45	20
Louisiana	10	1812; 1845; 1852; 1861; 1864; 1868; 1879; 1898; 1913; 1921	1921	255,450	724	496
Maine	1	1820	1820	15,000	135	116(g)
Maryland	4	1776; 1851; 1864; 1867	1867	35,500	181	143
Massachusetts	1	1780	1780	36,000	108	91
Michigan	4	1835; 1850; 1908; 1963	1964	19,867	8	4
Minnesota	1	1858	1858	20,000	182	96
Mississippi	4	1817; 1832; 1869; 1890	1890	25,742	104	35
Missouri	4	1820; 1865; 1875; 1945	1945	33,260	45	28
Montana	1	1889	1889	28,000	57	37
Nebraska	2	1866; 1875	1875	23,170	197	129
Nevada	1	1864	1864	17,160	110	65
New Hampshire	2	1776; 1784(h)	1784	12,200	135(h)	61(h)
New Jersey	3	1776; 1844; 1947	1947	16,040	21	16
New Mexico	1	1911	1912	26,136	175	82
New York	6	1777; 1801; 1821; 1846; 1868; 1894	1894	47,000	240	179
North Carolina	3	1776; 1868; 1970	1971	17,000	0	0
North Dakota	1	1889	1889	31,470	(c)	86

TABLE 2 (Cont.)

State or other jurisdiction	Number of constitutions	Dates of adoption	Effective date of present constitution	Estimated length (number of words)	Number of Amendments Proposed	Adopted
Ohio	2	1802; 1851	1851	29,110	184	103
Oklahoma	1	1907	1907	63,213	184	79
Oregon	1	1859	1859	23,000	256	127
Pennsylvania	4	1776; 1790; 1838; 1873; 1968(i)	1873; 1968	24,750	122	92
Rhode Island	1	1843(d)	1843	21,040	70	36
South Carolina	6	1776; 1778; 1790; 1865; 1868; 1895	1895	45,740	401	398
South Dakota	1	1889	1889	30,290	156	78
Tennessee	3	1796; 1835; 1870	1870	15,150	34	18
Texas	5	1845; 1861; 1866; 1869; 1876	1876	52,270	321	201
Utah	1	1896	1896	20,990	99	56
Vermont	3	1777; 1786; 1793	1793	7,600	200	44
Virginia	6	1776; 1830; 1851; 1868; 1902; 1970	1971	8,000	0	0
Washington	1	1889	1889	26,930	95	54
West Virginia	2	1863; 1872	1872	22,970	67	40
Wisconsin	1	1848	1848	17,900	121(j)	93(k)
Wyoming	1	1890	1890	23,170	61	33
Puerto Rico	1	1952	1952	9,000	7	6

(a) Total number of measures proposed by the Legislature, including duplications.

(b) Total number of proposed measures adopted by the Legislature, six of which require voter approval.

(c) Data not available.

(d) Colonial charters with some alterations, in Connecticut (1638, 1662) and Rhode Island (1663), served as the first constitutions for these States.

(e) 47, 1 and 12 prior amendments were incorporated in the constitution in 1955, 1961 and 1965 respectively.

(f) Three amendments were adopted but were nullified on procedural grounds by the Iowa Supreme Court.

(g) One adopted amendment will not become effective until the Legislature enacts further legislation.

(h) The constitution of 1784 was extensively amended, rearranged and clarified in 1793. Figures show proposals and adoptions since 1793.

(i) Limited convention.

(j) Separate ballot proposals, some concerning more than one section.

(k) Two of the ratified amendments were later invalidated by the Wisconsin Supreme Court.

Source: THE BOOK OF THE STATES 1972-73 (Chicago: Council of State Governments, 1972), p. 21.

—It would be throughout consistent with the U. S. Constitution.
—It would provide the basis for state government through a
   balanced governmental organization.
—It would express the possibilities of state power in positive
   terms.
—It would contain a statement to guarantee personal rights.
—It would include an orderly and reasonably easy amendment
   procedure.
—It would be restricted to fundamentals and would employ only
   clear, simple language.

Concern with an ideal state constitution does not stop with
agreement on basic characteristics. Beginning at least with the
publication of the first edition of the *Model State Constitution* in
1921 by the National Municipal League, the attention of the public
and of state officials themselves has been called repeatedly to the
specifics of a model constitutional document. The *Model State
Constitution* is now in its sixth edition, that version appearing in
1963.

The *Model State Constitution* recognizes that there is no model
state for it to be adopted by; indeed it was bypassed by the only
two states to have been created since its compilation, Alaska and
Hawaii. But it, like the Declaration of Independence as Lincoln
saw it, was not intended so much to be adopted but to serve as a
"standard maxim . . . which should be familiar to all . . . constantly looked at, constantly labored for, and even though never
perfectly attained, constantly approximated."[22]

The sixth edition goes back to the early state constitutions and
the United States Constitution for its model. It is short and simply
stated; it is couched in enabling, not inhibiting, language; it elimi-
nates most of the ephemeral provisions that properly belong in
statutes instead of in the fundamental law; and it is "unencum-
bered by any limitations, checks, or 'compensatory devices' not
likely to be needed."[23]

The *Model State Constitution,* as the selected bibliography
appended to this essay attests, is only one of the many helps
provided by the National Municipal League in the movement

toward improved state constitutions. Critically absent, however, is *public* conviction of the need to launch the movement in the first place. Perhaps one factor that inhibits the development of that conviction is apathy, an ignorance of the need; another, the lack of an effective group in most states to get the movement started; a third, the fact that by virtually overlooking the constitution it has been possible to obtain satisfactory results in terms of governmental performance, so that pressure for change builds up more slowly. There are undoubtedly other factors. A major factor inhibiting a fuller swing to constitutional revision, however, may be the fact that constitutional conventions themselves come under sharp criticism. They may not always be accurately representative of the states' people and interests; voting turnouts at state elections are never very good in any case, and constitutional convention questions often do as poorly as any item on the ballot. They are often partisan, not only in membership, but in the conduct of the convention's business. This partisanship is not always overt. Because of the prevailing conviction in America that constitutional conventions concern the people's work and thus place greater demands on the delegates, the demand is often made that convention delegates be nonpartisan. But "This demand makes it possible for political parties to disclaim any responsibility for the actions of the convention while at the same time exercising considerable power over the deliberations. The result is power without responsibility."[24]

The conventions often lack effective leadership, but just as frequently come under the domination of one group or person. As John Bebout has observed, "The organization and conduct of a 'successful' or useful constitutional convention does not simply happen. It requires administrative and political statesmanship, endowed with foresight, a conviction of the special public importance of the enterprise, and a sense of purpose and direction. Too many conventions have failed to live up to their high calling because they were organized and conducted much too casually."[25] They are notoriously open to the claims of special interests and to the persuasion of ambitious men. They are *ad hoc* affairs and meet only for a short time—six months is a long session. The time limitation at least works against the delegation developing a concern for simplification. They often do not appreciate the special problems involved in drafting constitutional revisions as opposed to those involved in legislative drafting. And conventions are an added expense which must be borne by the taxpayer.

Moreover, the record of adoption of the product of the state constitutional conventions is not good. In fact, the repeated demonstration in state after state of the practical difficulties in getting a revised constitution adopted by the voters is more than sufficient reason to try to secure constitutional change via the piecemeal amendment process, which is still the preferred method. One can only speculate on why voters do not want to approve constitutional changes. The traditional long ballot and voter fatigue undoubtedly have something to do with it; confusion with the national constitution is probably another factor; and the complexity of many of the proposed amendments may dismay voters. But the chief reason seems to be that suggested changes threaten one or more groups, who, when acting in concert, can defeat the best of proposed documents, even as they did the proposed Maryland constitution in 1961.

Thus, when Senator James H. Saunders of Delaware was first exposed to the emotions of those who might be affected by constitutional revision in a public hearing, he thought he had descended "into Hell." The members of the convention, he wrote, were accused by the public, depending on which provision was up for consideration, of being "bigoted, prejudiced, agnostic, atheistic, subversive, perverted, secretive, dictatorial, deceptive, and treacherous. And if you think those are strong words, you should hear what the people who didn't like our proposals said."[25] When a revised document comes to the voters, they are apt to carry such attitudes with them into the polling booth. In the abortive attempt to revise Kentucky's constitution in 1964-1966, for example, the strongest opposition was encountered from local government officials whose constitutional positions would have been altered by the proposed new document. With them in the vanguard, "The proposed constitution was rejected by an overwhelming majority of Kentucky voters, with more than a ten to

one negative vote in many counties and no lower than a two to
one negative vote in any county." As one comment on the election concluded, "the lack of popular appeal of many [of the]
reform dogmas" embodied in the proposed constitution was
amply demonstrated.[27] In the absence of citizen organizations to
get better voter understanding of the issues in many states, the
Kentucky case is replicated in a sizable proportion of the approval
elections held in recent years.

Constitutional conventions have by now become quite stylized.
In most states (see Table 3), the legislature is free to decide when
and how to call a convention into being, and with few exceptions
the question of a constitutional convention must be approved by
the voters. In several states, legislative discretion is restricted by a
constitutional mandate requiring periodic submission to the voters
the question of whether to call a convention. Recently, because
in practice legislatures have not always followed such a constitutional mandate, there has developed a demand to make an executive officer responsible for submitting the question at stated inter-
vals. After it is determined to have a convention, the next step is
the election of delegates, which is universally done by the voters
of the state concerned, the units of election most often being
state legislative districts. Once they meet (and most state constitutions provide considerable procedural detail for the convening and
operation of constitutional conventions), they usually work as
a single body. They are always restricted to the one function of
revising or writing a new constitution, and their members serve
only for the duration of the convention, having no further role
once the convention is adjourned. The product of a constitutional
convention in most states is often required to be adopted by an ex-
traordinary majority of the convention delegates (though the current tendency is toward a simple majority) and in most states must
be approved by the voters.

In the twentieth century, so-called "limited" conventions have
been utilized. These conventions are at the outset denied authority to engage in complete revision, having either been prohibited
by their enabling authority (usually the legislature) from making
alterations in specific provisions of the constitution or limited to

TABLE 3
Procedures for Calling Constitutional Conventions

State or other jurisdiction	Vote required in Legislature(a)	Approval by two sessions	Referendum vote	Popular ratification of convention proposals
Alabama	Maj.	No	ME	ME
Alaska	Maj.(b)	No	MP	MP
Arizona	Maj.	No	MP	MP
Arkansas	Maj.(c)	No	MP	MP
California	2/3	No	MP	MP
Colorado	2/3	No	MP	ME
Connecticut	2/3(b)	No	ME	ME
Delaware	2/3	No	MP	X
Florida	(d)	...	MP	MP
Georgia	2/3	No	None	MP
Hawaii	Maj.(b)	No	MP	MP(e)
Idaho	2/3	No	MP	MP
Illinois	3/5(b)	No	(f)	MP
Indiana	Maj.(c)	No	MP	MP
Iowa	Maj.(b)	No	MP	MP
Kansas	2/3	No	MP	X
Kentucky	Maj.	Yes	MP(g)	X
Louisiana	Maj.(c)	No	MP	X
Maine	2/3	No	None	ME
Maryland	Maj.(b)	No	ME	MP
Massachusetts	Maj.(c)	No	MP	X
Michigan	Maj.(b)	No	MP	MP
Minnesota	2/3	No	ME	(h)
Mississippi	Maj.	No	None	X
Missouri	Maj.(b)	No	MP	MP
Montana	2/3	No	MP	ME
Nebraska	3/5	No	MP(i)	MP
Nevada	2/3	No	ME	X
New Hampshire	Maj.(b)	No	MP	(j)
New Jersey	Maj.(k)	No	MP	MP
New Mexico	2/3	No	MP	MP
New York	Maj.(b)	No	MP	MP
North Carolina	2/3	No	ME	X
North Dakota	Maj.(l)	No	MP	ME
Ohio	2/3(b)	No	MP	MP
Oklahoma	(b)	No	MP	MP
Oregon	Maj.	No	MP	X
Pennsylvania	Maj.(c)	No	MP	MP
Rhode Island	Maj.(c)	No	MP	MP
South Carolina	2/3	No	ME	X
South Dakota	2/3	No	ME	X

TABLE 3   (Cont.)

State or other jurisdiction	Procedure for calling constitutional convention			Popular ratification of convention proposals
	Vote required in Legislature(a)	Approval by two sessions	Referendum vote	
Tennessee	Maj.(m)	No	MP	MP
Texas	Maj.(c)	No	MP	MP
Utah	2/3	No	ME	ME
Vermont	Maj.(c)	No	MP	Y
Virginia	2/3	No	MP	X
Washington	2/3	No	ME	ME
West Virginia	Maj.	No	ME	ME
Wisconsin	Maj.	No	MP	X
Wyoming	2/3	No	ME	Y
Puerto Rico	2/3	No	MP	MP

ME—Majority voting election.

MP—Majority voting on the proposition.

X—There appears to be no constitutional or general statutory provision for the submission of convention proposals to the electorate in these States, but in practice the Legislature may provide by statute for popular ratification of convention proposals in specific instances.

Y—Popular ratification required but no provision for size of vote.

(a) The entries in this column refer to the percentage of elected members in each house required to initiate the procedure for calling a constitutional convention.

(b) The question of calling a convention must be submitted to the electorate every 10 years in Alaska, Hawaii, Iowa, New Hampshire; every 16 years in Michigan; every 20 years in Connecticut, Illinois, Maryland, Missouri, New York, Ohio and Oklahoma.

(c) In the following States, the constitution does not provide for the calling of a constitutional convention. Legislative authority to call such a convention has been established in practice in Arkansas, Indiana, Louisiana and Texas by court decisions and precedents; in Pennsylvania by statute; in Rhode Island by advisory opinion of the court; and in Vermont by the opinion of the Attorney General. In Massachusetts the Legislature exercised an unchallenged assumption of this power.

(d) The power to call a convention is reserved to petition by the people.

(e) Majority must be 35 percent of total votes cast at general election; or at a special election, the majority must be 30 percent of the number of registered voters.

(f) Majority voting in election or 3/5 voting on issue.

(g) Must equal 1/4 of qualified voters at last general election.

(h) 3/5 voting on question.

(i) Must be 35 percent of total votes cast at election.

(j) 2/3 voting on question.

(k) The constitution does not provide for the calling of a constitutional convention. A convention was called however by legislation which was submitted to the people in referendum.

(l) The 1969 Legislature proposed an amendment to the constitution to provide for the calling of a constitutional convention. The amendment was adopted.

(m) The convention may not be held more than once in six years.

Source: THE BOOK OF THE STATES 1972-1973 (Chicago: Council of State Governments, 1972), p. 24.

making changes only in specified areas of constitutional concern. The New Jersey constitutional convention of 1947, for example, was expressly prohibited from altering the apportionment of legislative seats. Legal experts are far from agreement as to the extent a legislature can limit a convention's power. The Alaska constitution (Article XIII, sec. 4) goes so far as to deny the legislature the power to limit the powers of a constitutional convention. But limited conventions "appear to have been used to break log jams of unrelated constitutional problems needing attention. The limited convention [may also] prove to be an effective device to deal with the relatively non-controversial issue of simplification."[28]

Though amendment and constitutional conventions remain the formal, official methods of securing state constitutional change, some mention must be made of constitutional commissions. An increasing number of states call on commissions as auxiliaries in the constitutional revision process. Essentially staff bodies, these extraconstitutional and extralegal bodies are called on for advice and recommendation. "The popularity of these bodies is attributable largely to their general acceptability to state legislators, who may accept, reject, or modify in whole or in part commission recommendations."[29] Use of such bodies may increase still further as the advantage of removing constitutional revision from the full heat of factional politics and instead making it the product of informed study and debate comes to be realized.

Finally, it should be noted that a few state constitutions, including the Florida and Oregon constitutions, and several state court rulings, authorize the state legislature to prepare and propose an entire constitution for approval by the voters, thus bypassing both convention and commission altogether.

> When a Legislature proposes a revised or new constitution, whether assisted by a constitutional commission or not, in effect it is performing the same basic function as a constitutional convention—initiating, drafting, and proposing modifications in the basic law. But legislators, unlike delegates to a constitutional convention, are members of a governmental organism that is subject to constitutional mandates and restraints in conducting the ongoing affairs of the State. Thus,

legislators as constitution-makers make decisions on issues and
matters that often concern their own official position, relations,
and functions.[30]

A recent trend in state constitutional revision is revision by
stages. California provides the leading example of this development. A state Constitution Revision Commission created in 1963
first presented a set of proposals to the legislature revising the
basic general structure of state government. These were adapted
by the legislature and referred to the voters in 1966. Then a series
of other changes followed, before the commission presented its
final report in 1971, and some were passed by the legislature and
approved by the people. South Carolina and Nebraska subsequently began to employ the same method.

Such developments reflect persistent recognition of the need
for action. That need is not lessening. "Seldom have the
states of the Union faced such urgent demands for solution of
difficult problems, or had such challenging opportunities for con-
structive action," begins the report of the Committee for Economic Development in 1967. There is massive evidence around
us that states have not found solutions to problems ranging from
pollution to crime, from education to welfare, from meeting
recreation needs to providing adequate protection for their citizens' basic rights. At least since President Nixon took office
in 1969, the states have increasingly been offered opportunities
to assume a greater share of the burden of providing governmental
services under what President Nixon likes to call "the new
federalism."

The problem is that so many states are not equipped to solve
the problems before them or to seize the opportunities presented
to them. They are not up to those possibilities because state
government is generally weak and incompetent. How it got that
way is complex.[31] The need in any case is not to explain how but
to extricate the states from their dilemma. There is universal
agreement that the greatest help to that end would be to replace
their archaic constitutions, which shackle the states in most attempts to meet their present crises. Recent decades have seen

mounting interest in constitutional improvement and, as already
suggested, an increasing recourse to constitutional conventions.
Some successes have been achieved, but there is still a long way
to go. In years ahead there will necessarily be continuing em-
phasis on constitutional revision and consequently on constitutional conventions. The documents described in the pages that
follow will be of immense use in providing that base of public
understanding which is going to be necessary to enable the progress demanded.   RICHARD H. LEACH
                                   Durham, North Carolina
                                   February 1973

NOTES

1. See Francis D. Wormuth, *The Origins of Modern Constitutionalism* (New York: Harper, 1949), especially chapter 1.
2. Thomas A. Bailey, *The American Pageant,* 3d ed. (Boston: D. C. Heath, 1966), pp. 13-14.
3. Eugene P. Dvorin and Arthur J. Misner, *Governments Within the States* (Reading, Mass.: Addison-Wesley Publishing Co., 1971), p. 6.
4. *Proceedings and Debates of the Virginia State Convention of 1829-30* (Richmond: Ritchie and Cook, 1830), p. 53.
5. John L. O'Sullivan, *The United States Magazine and Democratic Review,* October 1837, Introduction.
6. Thomas Jefferson, *Notes on the State of Virginia* (Boston: Wells and Lilly, 1829), p. 123.
7. Albert L. Sturm, *Major Constitutional Issues in West Virginia* (Morgantown, W. Va.: Bureau for Government Research, West Virginia University, 1961), p. 10.
8. Ibid., p. 4.
9. Daniel R. Grant and H. C. Nixon, *State and Local Government in America,* 2d ed. (Boston: Allyn & Bacon, 1968), p. 120, quoting Lasswell from his famous *Politics: Who Gets What When, How.*
10. Grant and Nixon, op. cit., p. 121.
11. The phrase of John E. Bebout in his introduction to the sixth edition of *Model State Constitution* (1963).
12. See the article by Frank S. Adams, "New York Needs a New Constitution," *The New York Times,* February 13, 1967, p. 32.
13. Dvorin and Misner, *Governments Within the States,* op. cit., p. 6.
14. Roger Sherman Hoar, quoted in Robert A. Shanley, *The Problems of Simplifying the Massachusetts Constitution* (Amherst, Mass.: Bureau of Government Research, University of Massachusetts, 1966), p. 18.

15. The Commission on Intergovernmental Relations, *A Report to the President for Transmittal to Congress* (Washington, D. C.: Government Printing Office, 1955), pp. 37, 56.
16. Quoted in *Report of the North Carolina State Constitution Study* (Raleigh, 1968), p. 1.
17. New York: McGraw-Hill, 1966.
18. New York: Committee for Economic Development, 1967.
19. *The Book of the States 1972-73* (Chicago: Council of State Governments, 1972), p. 3.
20. Ibid.
21. See David Fellman, "What Should a State Constitution Contain?", in W. Brooke Graves, ed., *Major Problems in State Constitutional Revision* (Chicago: Public Administration Service, 1960).
22. From Lincoln's Speech in Springfield, Ill., June 26, 1857, reprinted in John G. Nicolay and John Hay, eds., *Complete Works of Abraham Lincoln* (New York: Francis D. Tandy, 1905), vol. 2, p. 331.
23. John E. Bebout, Introduction to the sixth edition, *Model State Constitution,* op. cit., p. x.
24. Alan K. Campbell, "A New Constitution for New York?", *Proceedings of the Academy of Political Science* 28: 3 (January 1967).
25. John E. Bebout, "Organizing the Constitutional Convention," *Proceedings of the Academy of Political Science* 28: 22 (January 1967).
26. James H. Saunders, "A Former Senator's 'Unconstitutional' Remarks on Constitutional Revision," *State Government,* Winter 1970, p. 64.
27. Grant and Nixon, *State and Local Government in America,* op. cit., p. 149.
28. *The Problem of Simplifying the Mississippi Constitution,* p. 30.
29. *Book of the States 1972-73,* p. 7.
30. Ibid., p. 10.
31. For one answer see Sanford, *Storm Over the States,* op. cit., chapter III.

SELECTED READING

BAKER, GORDON E., *State Constitutions: Reapportionment* (New York: National Municipal League, 1960).

BEBOUT, JOHN E. and MAY, JANICE, *The Texas Constitution: Problems and Prospects for Revision* (Arlington, Tex.: Institute of Urban Studies, The University of Texas at Arlington, 1971).

BRADEN, GEORGE D. and COHN, RUBIN G., The Illinois Constitution: An Annotated and Comparative Analysis (Urbana, Ill.: Institute of Government and Public Affairs, University of Illinois, 1969).

BURDINE, J. ALTON, "Basic Materials for the Study of State Constitutions and State Constitutional Development," *American Political Science Review* 48: 1140-1152 (December 1954).

CLEM, ALAN L., ed., *Contemporary Approaches to State Constitutional Revision* (Vermillion, S. D.: Governmental Research Bureau, The University of South Dakota, 1970).

DEALEY, JAMES Q., *Growth of American State Constitutions from 1776 to the End of the Year 1914* (Boston: Ginn and Co., 1915).

DISHMAN, ROBERT B., *State Constitutions: The Shape of the Document*, Rev. ed. (New York: National Municipal League, 1968).

DOVELL, J. E., *Modernizing State Constitutions* (Gainesville, Fla.: Public Administration Clearing Service, University of Florida, 1950).

EDWARDS, WILLIAM A., ed., *Index Digest of State Constitutions*, 2d ed. (New York: Oceana Publications, 1959).

GOVE, SAMUEL K. and RANNEY, VICTORIA, eds., *Con-Con: Issues for the Illinois Constitutional Convention* (Urbana, Ill.: University of Illinois Press, 1970).

GRAD, FRANK P., *The State Constitution: Its Function and Form for Our Time* (New York: National Municipal League, 1968).

GRAVES, W. BROOKE, ed., *Major Problems in State Constitutional Revision* (Chicago: Public Administration Service, 1960).

HALEVY, BALFOUR J., comp. (with supplement by Fink, Myron, comp.), "A Selective Bibliography on State Constitutional Revision," 2d ed. (New York: National Municipal League, 1967).

LEACH, RICHARD H., ed., *Compacts of Antiquity: State Constitutions* (Atlanta: Southern Newspaper Publishers Association Foundation, 1969).

MILLER, JAMES NATHAN, "Dead Hand of the Past," *National Civic Review*, April 1968, pp. 183-188.

STATE CONSTITUTIONAL CONVENTION STUDIES (New York: National Municipal League, 1969–): Number 1—Rhode Island, 1969; Number 2—Pennsylvania, 1969; Number 3—Maryland, 1970; Number 4—New Jersey, 1970; Number 5—Hawaii, 1971; Number 6—Missouri, 1971.

STURM, ALBERT L. *Constitution-Making in Michigan, 1961-1962* (Ann Arbor: Institute of Public Administration, University of Michigan, 1963).

——— . *Major Constitutional Issues in West Virginia* (Morgantown, W. Va.: Bureau for Government Research, West Virginia University, 1961).

——— . *Methods of State Constitutional Reform* (Ann Arbor: Institute of Public Administration, University of Michigan, 1954).

——— . *Thirty Years of State Constitution-Making, 1938-1968* (Williamsburg, Va.: Marshall-Wythe School of Law, College of William and Mary, 1971).

"SYMPOSIUM ON CONSTITUTIONAL REVISION," *West Virginia Law Review* 71:237-325 (April and June 1969).

WHEELER, JOHN P., Jr., *The Constitutional Convention: A Manual on Its Planning, Organization and Operation* (New York: National Municipal League, 1961).

——— , ed., *Salient Issues of Constitutional Revision* (New York: National Municipal League, 1961).

State
Constitutional
Conventions

Alabama

[Al 1]
Alabama (Ter.) Convention, 1819.
Journal of the convention of the Alabama Territory, begun July 5, 1819. Huntsville, 1819. [Washington, D. C., 1909]
40 p.

"Photofacsimile reprint, 57 copies only."
Convention adjourned August 2, 1819; Alabama admitted to the Union December 14, 1819.

[Al 2]
Alabama (Ter.) Convention, 1819.
Memorial of the convention of the people of the state of Alabama, assembled to form a constitution and state government, praying that a part of West Florida may be annexed to said state. February 22, 1821. Printed by order of the Senate of the United States. Washington, 1821.
4 p. ([U. S.] 16th Cong., 2d sess. Senate. Doc. 109)

[Al 3]
Alabama. Constitution.
Constitution of the state of Alabama.

(In Alabama. Laws, statutes, etc. A digest of the laws. 1823. p. 914-934.)

Also issued as (U. S.) 16th Cong., 1st sess. House. Doc. 1.

[Al 4]
Alabama. Convention, 1861.
Ordinances adopted by the people of the state of Alabama, in convention, at Montgomery, commencing on the seventh day of January, 1861. Andrew B. Moore, governor; William M. Brooks, president of the convention. Montgomery, 1861.
30, [1] p.

Resolutions adopted by the people of the state of Alabama, in convention, at Montgomery, commencing on the seventh day of January, 1861 (p. [27]-30) has special title page.

[Al 5]
Alabama. Constitution.
Ordinances and constitution of the state of Alabama, with the constitution of the provisional government and of the Confederate States of America. Montgomery, 1861.
152 p.

[Al 6]
Alabama. Convention, 1861.
The history and debates of the convention of the people of Alabama, begun and held in the city of Montgomery, on the seventh day of January, 1861; in which is preserved the speeches of the secret sessions and many valuable state papers. By William R. Smith, one of the delegates from Tuscaloosa. Montgomery, 1861.
v p., 1 l., [9]-464.

[Al 7]
Alabama. Constitutional Convention, 1865.
Journal of the proceedings of convention of the state of Alabama, held in the city of Montgomery, on Tuesday, September 12, 1865. Benjamin Fitzpatrick, president of convention, Wm. H. Osborne, secretary of convention, W. W. Screws, assistant secretary of convention. Montgomery, 1865.
88 p.

"Message of Governor Lewis E. Parsons": p. [3]-9.

[Al 8]
Alabama. Constitution.

The constitution and ordinances, adopted by the state convention of Alabama, which assembled at Montgomery, on the twelfth day of September, A.D. 1865; with index, analysis, and table of titles; by J. W. Shepherd. Montgomery, 1865.

vii, [9]-80 p.

[Al 9]
Alabama. Constitutional Convention, 1867.

Official journal of the constitutional convention of the state of Alabama, held in the city of Montgomery, commencing on Tuesday, November 5, A.D. 1867. Montgomery, 1868.

291, [1] p.

[Al 10]
Alabama. Constitutional Convention, 1867.

Ordinances [and resolutions] of state convention [held in the city of Montgomery, commencing November 5, 1867]

(In Alabama. Laws, statutes, etc. Acts of the sessions of July, September, and November, 1868 . . . Montgomery, 1868-[1869] p. [161]-194)

[Al 11]
Alabama. Constitution.

Letter of E.W. Peck, president of the constitutional convention of Alabama, communicating a copy of the constitution of the state of Alabama as revised and amended by the convention assembled at Montgomery on the 5th day of November, 1867. February 24, 1868. Referred to the Committee on the Judiciary and ordered to be printed. [Washington, D. C.?, 1868?]

19 p. ([U.S.] 40th Cong., 2d sess. Senate. Misc. Doc. 32)

Caption title.

[Al 12]
Alabama. Constitution.
    Constitution of the state of Alabama, as revised and amended
by the convention assembled at Montgomery, on the fifth of
November, 1867. Montgomery, 1867.
    24 p.

[Al 13]
Alabama. Legislature. Joint Special Committee.
    Report.

    (In Alabama. Legislature. Journal of the Senate . . . commenc-
ing November 16, 1874. Montgomery, 1875. p. 296-305)

    "The joint committee . . . to which were referred . . . the
several bills . . . having in view the amendment of the Constitution . . ."

[Al 14]
Alabama. Constitutional Convention, 1875.
    Journal of the constitutional convention of the state of
Alabama, assembled in the city of Montgomery September 6,
1875. Montgomery, 1875.
    231 p.

    "Constitution of the state of Alabama": p. [175]-211.

[Al 15]
Alabama. Constitutional Convention, 1901.
    Journal of the proceedings of the constitutional convention
of the state of Alabama, held in the city of Montgomery, commencing May 21, 1901. With an index prepared by the secretary.
Montgomery, 1901.
    1888 p.

[Al 16]
Alabama. Constitutional Convention, 1901.
    Official proceedings of the constitutional convention of the

[Al 16, cont.]
state of Alabama, May 21, 1901, to September 3, 1901 . . .
[Wetumpka, 1941]
    4 v. (5150 p.)

——. Index. St. Paul, [c1943].
    245 p.

——. Index, by George Huddleston, Jr., and James N.
Bloodworth. University, 1948.
    85 p.

[Al 17]
Alabama. Constitutional Convention, 1901.
    Rules of the constitutional convention, 1901, with lists of the
standing committees, the officers of the convention, and a roll of
the standing committees, the officers of the convention, and a
roll of the delegates. Montgomery, 1901.
    37 p. (State of Alabama. Constitutional convention, 1901. Doc. 3)

    Addenda: 2 numb. l. inserted.

[Al 18]
Cunningham, R. M.
    Speech of Hon. R. M. Cunningham (of Jefferson County) in
support of the majority report of the Committee on Suffrage and
Elections, in the constitutional convention of Alabama, July 27,
1901 . . . Montgomery, 1901.
    30 p. (Alabama. Constitutional convention, 1901. Doc. 8)

[Al 19]
Alabama. Constitution.
    Constitution of the state of Alabama, as adopted by the con-
stitutional convention, September 3, 1901, and in effect November 28, 1901. Montgomery, 1901.
    72 p.

    Caption title.

[Al 20]
Alabama. Constitution.
   Constitutions of 1875 and 1901. Paralleled, annotated and indexed by James J. Mayfield . . . [2d ed.] Montgomery, 1918.
   xxi p., 1 l., 355 p.

[Al 21]
Alabama. Governor, 1911-1915 (Emmet O'Neal).
   Constitutional convention; necessity for new constitution.
Message of Emmet O'Neal, governor, to the legislature of Alabama,
January 15, 1915. Montgomery, 1915.
   20 p. (Alabama. Legislature. Regular sess., 1915. Legislative
Doc. 3)

[Al 22]
Alabama. Constitution.
   Amendments to the constitution of the state of Alabama
(1901). Annotated and proposed amendments rejected. Prepared
by N. H. Seay . . . [Montgomery] 1923.
   19 p.

[Al 23]
Alabama. Constitution.
   Alabama constitution, annotated; a complete digest of all decisions by the Supreme Court of Alabama construing the constitution of Alabama as amended, including constitution of 1901 with
apposite provisions of previous constitutions of 1819, 1861, 1865,
1868, 1875, by Thomas E. Skinner . . . [Birmingham, c1938]
   [8], 1054 p.

[Al 24]
Alabama. Constitution.
   The constitution of the state of Alabama and amendments.
Alexander City, 1954.
   190 p. (Publication of the Alabama State Dept. of Archives
and History. Historical and patriotic series, 16)

[Al 25]
Alabama. Legislative Reference Service.
Synopses of constitutional amendments proposed by the legislature at its 1957 regular session. Montgomery, 1957.
7 numb. l.

Caption title.

Alaska

[Ak 1]
Alaska (Ter.) Statehood Committee.
Handbook for delegates to the Alaska constitutional convention, convened at College, Alaska, November 8, 1955. [n. p., 1955]
[1] i, 14 numb. l.

Cover title.
"An act to provide for the holding of a constitutional convention . . . ": [6] p. inserted at end.

[Ak 2]
Alaska (Ter.) Constitutional Convention, 1955-1956.
Minutes of the daily proceedings, Alaska constitutional convention, University of Alaska, 1955-1956, College, Alaska . . .
Juneau, 1965.
6 pts.

Parts 1-5 paged continuously.
Appendices:—I. Enabling legislation: chapter 46, session laws of Alaska, 1955.—II. Address: the Honorable E. L. Bartlett, delegate to Congress (November 8, 1955)—III. Address: the Honorable Ernest Gruening, former governor of Alaska, 1939-1953 (November 9, 1955)—IV. Address: the Honorable George H. Lehleitner, a private citizen of New Orleans, Louisiana (January 23, 1956)—V. Committee proposals and commentary.—VI. Constitution of the state of Alaska.

[Ak 3]
Alaska (Ter.) Constitutional Convention, 1955-1956.
. . . Report of the Committee on Judiciary Branch. [Juneau?
1955]
7, 8 numb. l.

Caption title.
At head of title: Constitutional convention. Committee pro-
posal/2, December 5, 1955.
Contents:—Article on the judiciary.—Commentary on the
judiciary article.

[Ak 4]
Alaska (Ter.) Constitutional Convention, 1955-1956.
Proposed constitution for the state of Alaska; a report to the
people of Alaska from the Alaska constitutional convention,
College, Alaska, February, 1956 . . . Juneau [1956]
folder (8 p.)

[Ak 5]
Alaska. Constitution.
The constitution of the state of Alaska, agreed upon by the
delegates of the people of Alaska, February 5, 1956. [Fairbanks,
1956]
55 p.

Arizona

[Az 1]
Arizona (Ter.) Constitutional Convention, 1891.
Journals of the constitutional convention for the state of
Arizona. Convention convened September 7, 1891, and adjourned
October 3, 1891. Phoenix, 1891.
59 p.

[Az 2]
Arizona (Ter.) Constitutional Convention, 1891.
Constitution for the state of Arizona, as adopted by the constitutional convention, Friday, October 2, 1891, and address to the
people of the territory. Phoenix, 1891.
28 p.

[Az 3]
Arizona (Ter.) Constitution.
Admission of Arizona into the Union. [With constitution for
the state of Arizona adopted by the constitutional convention
October 2, 1891] November 3, 1893. Committed to the Committee of the Whole House on the State of the Union and ordered to
be printed. Mr. Smith of Arizona, from the Committee on Territories, submitted the following report (to accompany H. R. 4393)
[Washington? 1893?]
30 p. (U. S.] 53d Cong., 1st sess. House Rept. 168)

Caption title.

[Az 4]
Arizona (Ter.) Constitutional Convention, 1910.
... Journals of the constitutional convention of Arizona as pro-
vided for by the enabling act of Congress approved June 20, 1910.
Held in the hall of the House of Representatives in the Capitol of
the territory of Arizona, at Phoenix, October 10 to December 9,
1910. Compiled by Con P. Cronin, state librarian of Arizona.
November 1, 1925. [Phoenix? 1925]
    1 p. l. 648 numb. l., 1 l.

[Az 5]
Arizona (Ter.) Constitutional Convention, 1910.
Minutes of the constitutional convention of the territory of
Arizona. Session began on the tenth day of October, A. D. 1910,
Phoenix, Arizona. Phoenix [1910]
    449 p.

[Az 6]
Arizona (Ter.) Constitutional Convention, 1910.
The proposed constitution for the state of Arizona. Adopted
by the constitutional convention, held at Phoenix, Ariz., from
October 10 to December 9, 1910. [Phoenix? 1910]
    40 p.

    Caption title.
    Although accepted by Congress, this constitution was vetoed
by President Taft because of its provision for the recall of judges.

[Az 7]
Arizona. Constitution.
Constitutional amendments submitted to the people by the
legislature, and those proposed by initiative petition of the people,
and acts passed at the regular and first special sessions of the first
state legislature, 1912, against which referendums were filed, all
of which were approved by the qualified electors of the state at
the election held on November fifth, 1912, and became laws on

[Az 7, cont.]
the proclamation of the governor, issued on December the fifth,
1912 . . . [Phoenix, 1912]
    2 p. l., 41 p.

The people of Arizona ratified an amendment on December 12,
1911, which removed from the constitution the provision on
judicial recall. After Arizona was admitted as a state to the Union,
the provision on recall of judges was restored to the constitution
on November 5, 1912.

[Az 8]
Arizona. Constitution.
    Constitution of the state of Arizona, adopted by the constitu-
tional convention held at Phoenix, October 10–December 9, 1910,
and ratified by the people at an election held February 9, 1911.
Including all amendments and the text of all superseded provisions.
Annotated to July 14, 1939. Phoenix, 1939.
    138 p. (Arizona newsletter, published by the State Depts. of
Library and Archives . . . no. 11, July 1939)

[Az 9]
Arizona. Constitution.
    Constitution of Arizona. Compiled and issued by Wesley Bolin,
secretary of state, and members of the 22d Legislature . . .
[Phoenix? 1961]
    2 p. l., 50 p.

Arkansas

[Ar 1]
Arkansas. Constitutional Convention, 1836.

Journal of the proceedings of the convention to form a constitution and system of state government for the people of Arkansas, at the session of the said convention held at Little Rock, in the territory of Arkansas, which commenced on the fourth day of January, and ended on the thirtieth day of January, one thousand eight hundred and thirty-six.

52, 8 p.

"Report. House of Representatives, Wednesday, October 14, 1835. The joint committee, on the part of the House of Representatives, to whom was referred so much of the Governor's message as relates to the subject of state government, in conjunction with the Committee on the part of the Legislative Council," p. [1]-6 at end.

"Minority report, House of Representatives, Wednesday, October 14, 1835 . . . ," p. [7]-8, at end.

[Ar 2]
Arkansas. Constitution.

Constitution done by the people of Arkansas, in convention assembled, at Little Rock one thousand eight hundred and thirty six. Little Rock, 1838.

23 p.

[Ar 3]
Arkansas. Convention, 1861.
Journal of both sessions of the convention of the state of Arkansas, which were begun and held at the Capitol, in the city of Little Rock. Published by authority. Little Rock, 1861.
509 p.

Page 228 to page 230 incorrectly numbered 128-130.
Contents:—An act to provide for a state convention.—Proclamation by the governor.—Journal, March 4-21, 1861.—Journal of the called session, May 6-June 3, 1861.—Appendix.

[Ar 4]
Arkansas. Constitutional Convention, 1864.
Journal of the convention of delegates of the people of Arkansas. Assembled at the Capitol, January 4, 1864; also journals of the House of Representatives of the sessions of 1864, 1864-1865, and 1865. By authority. Little Rock, 1870.
58, 309, 67 p.

[Ar 5]
Arkansas. Constitution.
Constitution of the state of Arkansas [1864. With ordinances of the convention which assembled January 4, 1864]

(In Arkansas. Laws, statutes, etc. New constitution, with the acts of the General Assembly . . . Little Rock, 1865. p. [5]-30)

[Ar 6]
Arkansas. Constitutional Convention, 1868.
Debates and proceedings of the convention which assembled at Little Rock, January 7, 1868 . . . to form a constitution for the state of Arkansas. Official: J. G. Price, secretary. Little Rock, 1868.
812, [5], [813-979] p.

Edited by James M. Pomeroy.
"Ordinances, public resolutions, & orders, passed, and memorials addressed to the Congress of the United States": p. [813]-848.
"The Constitution of the State of Arkansas": p. [849]-898.

[Ar 7]
Arkansas. Constitution.
The constitution of the state of Arkansas. Framed and adopted by the convention which assembled at Little Rock, January 7, 1868, and ratified by the registered electors of the state, at the election beginning March 13, 1868, with marginal notes, a full documentary history of the constitution, and a copious index. To which is prefixed the Constitution of the United States, with an index thereto. By James M. Pomeroy . . . By authority. Little Rock, 1870.
1 v. (various pagings)

[Ar 8]
Arkansas. Constitutional Convention, 1874.
Proceedings of the constitutional convention of the people of the state of Arkansas, convened at the Capitol, July 14, 1874.
2 v. (932 p.)

Caption title.
Manuscript copy.

[Ar 9]
Arkansas. Constitution.
The constitution of the state of Arkansas. Framed and adopted by the convention which assembled at Little Rock, July 14, 1874, and ratified by the people of the state, at the election held October 13, 1874. With marginal notes, a documentary history of the constitution, and a copious index, in the nature of a digest. By James M. Pomeroy. Little Rock, 1876.
1 v. (various pagings)

Members of the Arkansas constitutional convention of 1874, acts of General Assembly providing for convention to frame new constitution.—Abstract of votes.—Address to the people of the state, prepared by order of the constitutional convention, and proclamation by the State Board of Election Supervisors. p. 67-73.

[Ar 10]
Arkansas. Constitution.
Constitution of the state of Arkansas (with amendments)
Issued by Earle W. Hodges, secretary of state . . . [Little Rock?]
1911.
    73 p.

Cover title.
Proclamation by the State Board of Election Supervisors: p. 67-73.

[Ar 11]
Arkansas. Constitutional Convention, 1918.
Proposals of the committees of the constitutional convention
of Arkansas, to be presented to the convention at its meeting on
the first Monday in July, nineteen eighteen. Little Rock [1918]
    [3], 2-130 numb. l.

Cover title.
"Index . . .": [4] p. inserted.

[Ar 12]
**Arkansas. Constitutional Convention, 1918. Committee on Sub-
    mission and Address to the people.**
Address to the people of the state of Arkansas [and proposed
constitution. Little Rock, 1918?]
    31, [1] p.

[Ar 13]
Arkansas. Constitution.
Constitution of the state of Arkansas, with all amendments.
[Little Rock] 1958.
    116 p.

Cover title.

California

[Ca 1]
California. Constitutional Convention, 1849.
Report of the debates in the convention of California, on the formation of the state constitution, in September and October, 1849. By J. Ross Browne. Washington, 1850.
479, xlvi p., 1 l.

"Constitution of the State of California": p. [iii]-xiii.

[Ca 2]
California. Constitution.
Constitution of the state of California. San Francisco, 1849.
19 p.

"Address to the people of California": p. [17]-19.

[Ca 3]
California. Legislature. Senate.
Majority and minority reports of the Select Committee on the Constitution. [n. p., 1853?]
31 p. (Senate Doc. 16, sess. 1853)

Majority report signed by J. W. Coffroth, C. F. Lott. Minority reports signed by J. R. Snyder and H. A. Crabb.

[Ca 4]
California. Legislature. Senate.
Report of select committee [to whom was referred "amendments to the Constitution," and Senate and Assembly bills,
"recommending the people to vote for or against calling a convention to revise and change the entire Constitution of this
State." n. p., 1853?]
4 p. (Senate Doc. 56, sess. 1853)

Report signed by H. A. Crabb, J. H. Ralston, and J. H. Baird.

[Ca 5]
California. Legislature. Senate.
Report of the special committee to whom was referred the act
recommending to the electors to vote for or against a convention
to revise and change the constitution of this state, January, 1857.

(In appendix to Senate journal of the 8th session of the legislature of the state of California. Sacramento, 1857. 14 p.)

[Ca 6]
**California. Legislature. Joint Committee on Constitutional
Convention.**
Report. [Sacramento, 1874]
4 p.

Cover title: California report of constitutional convention 1874.

[Ca 7]
California. Legislature. Assembly.
Majority report of the Assembly Judiciary Committee on Assembly bill no. 236, to provide for calling a convention to revise
and change the constitution of this state. [n.p., 1875?]
8 p.

Signed McConnell, chairman, J. S. Chapman, J. E. Murphy,
J. J. Scrivner, J. McKenna, H. A. Carter, T. M. Swan, T. J. Clunie.

[Ca 8]
California. Legislature. Assembly.
Minority report of the Assembly Judiciary Committee on Assembly bill no. 236, to provide for calling a convention to revise and change the constitution of this state. [n. p., 1875?]
5 p.

Signed Archer, Harding, Carson, Harris.

[Ca 9]
California. Constitutional Convention, 1878-1879.
Debates and proceedings of the constitutional convention of the state of California, convened at the city of Sacramento, Saturday, September 28, 1878. E. B. Willis and P. K. Stockton, official stenographers. Sacramento, 1880-1881.
3 v.

The convention adjourned March 3, 1879.
"Constitution of the State of California": p. 1510-1521.

[Ca 10]
Bynon, A. A.
The constitutional convention 1878. State of California. San Francisco, 1878.
148 p.

On cover: Constitutional convention handbook.

[Ca 11]
California. Constitution.
The proposed constitution reviewed in an address to the reformers of California. [n. p., 1879?]
48 p.

Caption title.

[Ca 12]
California. Constitution.
The constitution of the state of California adopted in 1879, with references to similar provisions in the constitutions of other

[Ca 12, cont.]

states, and to the decisions of the courts of the United States, the Supreme Court of California, and the supreme courts of such other states as have constitutional provisions similar to those of California. To which is prefixed the Constitution of the United States and a parallel arrangement of the constitutions of 1863 and 1879. By Robert Desty. San Francisco, 1879.

431 p.

[Ca 13]
California. Legislature. Senate. Committee on Constitutional Amendments.

Report of the testimony and proceedings taken before the Senate Committee on constitutional amendments, relative to Senate constitutional amendment no. 8, abrogating provisions of constitution as to Railroad Commission, and placing distance tariff in constitution . . .

(In appendix to the journals of the Senate and Assembly of the 30th session of the legislature of the state of California. Sacramento, 1893. v. 8, x, 235 p.)

[Ca 14]
California. Constitution.

Summary of amendments to the constitution of California. Adopted by the legislature and approved by the voters, with statement of vote for and against each amendment 1883-1920. History of direct legislation 1912-1920. Initiative and referendum measures submitted to vote of electors. Compiled by Frank C. Jordan, secretary of state. Sacramento, 1921.

31 p. incl. tables.

[Ca 15]
California. Constitutional Commission.

Report. Submitted to the governor of California, December 29, 1930. [Sacramento, 1931]

93 p.

[Ca 16]
California. Legislature. Legislative Constitutional Revision
     Committee.
[Program, list of members, etc.] October 29-30, 1947.
Santa Barbara [1947]
     [10] p.

Act establishing committee inserted at front.

[Ca 17]
California. Legislature. Legislative Constitutional Revision
     Committee.
[Letters, proposals, etc.] October 4, 1967-August 9, 1948.
Santa Barbara, 1947-1948.
     20 nos. in 2 v.

[Ca 18]
California. Constitution.
     Constitution of the state of California, annotated 1946. Com-
piled by Paul Mason. Published by direction of the California
legislature. [Sacramento, c1946]
     1728 p.

"This edition of the Constitution is a revision of the annotated
edition of 1933. In addition to the court decisions, this edition
cites the opinions of the Attorney General . . . The Constitution
of 1849, the United States Constitution, and certain other historical documents are included, as in the earlier volume . . ."
Cf. Foreword.

———. Supplement to Mason's annotated constitution of California
1946. Compiled by Paul Mason. Amendments voted on at elections November 5, 1946, to November 7, 1950. Published by the
California legislature. Sacramento, 1951.
     39 p.

[Ca 19]

California. Governor's Lawyers Committee to Draft a Water Rights Constitutional Amendment.

An explanation of the Governor's Water Lawyers Committee draft of a water rights constitutional amendment, by Harold W. Kennedy . . . vice chairman, Governor's Water Lawyers Commitee. [Sacramento, 1957?]

26 numb. l.

Caption title.

[Ca 20]

California. Governor's Lawyers Committee Appointed to Draft a Water Rights Constitutional Amendment.

Report . . . Sacramento, 1957.

6, [3] l.

Caption title.

[Ca 21]

California. Governor's Lawyers Committee Appointed to Draft a Water Rights Constitutional Amendment.

Proposed water rights constitutional amendment (New sections 5 to 10, article XIV) [Sacramento] 1957.

11 numb. l.

Caption title.

[Ca 22]

California. Constitution.

Constitution of the United States, Declaration of Rights, Declaration of Independence, Articles of Confederation, constitution of the state of California as last amended in 1956. Act for the admission of California into the Union. Constitutional history of California. [Sacramento] 1958.

xxxi, 334 p., illus.

"Constitution of the State of California" appears first in title on some of the earlier editions.

——. Supplement . . . containing amendments adopted November 4, 1958. December 1958. [Sacramento, 1959]

15 p.

Colorado

[Col 1]
Colorado (Ter.) Constitutional Convention, 1864.
  Constitution and ordinances of the state of Colorado, adopted in convention, July 11, 1864, together with an address to the people of Colorado. Denver [1864?]
    1 p. l., [2]-19 p.

  The constitution framed by this convention on March 21, 1864, was rejected by the voters.

[Col 2]
Colorado (Ter.) Constitutional Convention, 1865.
  . . . Message of the President of the United States, transmitting a communication addressed to him by John Evans and J. B. Chaffee, as United States senators elect from the state of Colorado, and other information in relation to the admission of that state into the Union . . . [Washington, 1866]
    34 p. ([U. S.] 39th Cong., 1st sess. Senate. Ex. Doc. 10)

  Caption title.
  Running title: Admission of Colorado into the Union.
  "January 12, 1866. Read, referred to the Committee on Territories, and ordered to be printed, with accompanying documents."
  "Proceedings of Constitutional Convention": p. 4-31.

[Col 3]
Colorado (Ter.) Constitutional Convention, 1865.
 State constitution as adopted by the constitutional convention, August 12, 1865. To be submitted to the people of Colorado for adoption or rejection, on the first Tuesday of September, 1865 . . . [Denver? 1865]
  12, 3 p.

 "An address to the people of Colorado on the policy of adopting a state government": 3 p. at end.

[Col 4]
Colorado (Ter.) Committee of Citizens.
 Draft of a constitution published under the direction of a committee of citizens of Colorado for consideration and discussion by the citizens of the centennial state. Denver, 1875.
  xiii, 54, [1] p.

[Col 5]
Colorado (Ter.) Constitutional Convention, 1875-1876.
 Rules for the government of the convention to form a state constitution for the territory of Colorado; together with the enabling act authorizing said convention; also, the Constitution of the United States, with amendments thereto. Denver, 1876.
  39 p.

[Col 7]
Colorado (Ter.) Constitutional Convention, 1875-1876.
 Proceedings of the constitutional convention held in Denver, December 20, 1875, to frame a constitution for the state of Colorado, together with the enabling act passed by the Congress of the United States and approved March 3, 1875, the address to the people issued by the convention, the constitution as adopted, and the President's proclamation. Published by authority of Timothy O'Conner, secretary of state. Denver, 1907.
  778 p.

[Col 8]
Colorado (Ter.) Constitutional Convention, 1875-1876.
. . . Timber-lands of Colorado Territory. Memorial from the constitutional convention of Colorado, asking for the transfer of the timber-lands of said territory to its care and custody, and setting forth reasons therefore. [Washington, 1876]
4 p. ([U. S.] 44th Cong., 1st sess. House. Misc. Doc. 146)

Caption title.
Referred to the Committee on the Public Lands and ordered printed March 20, 1876.

[Col 9]
Colorado (Ter.) Constitutional Convention, 1875-1876.
Constitution . . . adopted in convention, March 14, 1876; also an address of the convention to the people of Colorado. Election, Saturday, July 1, 1876. Denver, 1876.
65 p.

[Col 10]
Colorado. Constitution.
The constitution of the state of Colorado, revised to May 1, 1958 . . . [Denver, 1958?]
102 p.

Published by authority of secretary of state.

Connecticut

[Ct 1]
Connecticut (Colony) Constitution, 1639.
  Fundamental orders of Connecticut 1638-1639.

  (In Thorpe, Francis Newton, comp. The federal and state constitutions, colonial charters, and other organic laws of the states,
territories, and colonies now or heretofore forming the United
States of America. Washington, 1909. v. 1, p. 519-523)

[Ct 2]
Connecticut (Colony) Charters.
  Charter of Connecticut—1662.

  (In Thorpe, Francis Newton, comp. The federal and state constitutions, colonial charters, and other organic laws of the states,
territories, and colonies now or heretofore forming the United
States of America. Washington, 1909. v. 1, p. 529-536)

The charter "was not regarded as a grant of new powers, but
as a formal recognition of the government already established by
the people and a confirmation of the rights and privileges they had
exercised from the first . . . The frame of government continued
to rest on the same broad foundation on which the Constitution
of 1639 had placed it."—J. Hammond Trumbull. Historical notes
on the constitution of Connecticut, 1639-1818. Hartford, 1873.
p. 10.

[Ct 3]
Connecticut. Laws, statutes, etc.
An act containing an abstract and declaration of the rights and privileges of the people of this state, and securing the same. [1784]

(In Poore, Ben. Perley, comp. The federal and state constitutions, colonial charters, and other organic laws of the United States. Washington, 1877. v. 1, p. 257-258)

This act, with an accompanying declaration, continued the Charter of 1662 in force as the organic law of the state.

[Ct 4]
Connecticut. Constitutional Convention, 1818.
Journal of the proceedings of the convention of delegates convened at Hartford, August 26, 1818, for the purpose of forming a constitution of civil government for the people of the state of Connecticut. Hartford, 1901.
121 p.

The constitution adopted in 1818 is included.

[Ct 5]
Connecticut. Constitution.
Amendments to the constitution [of 1818, ratified 1828, 1832, 1836, 1838, 1845, 1850, 1855, 1856, 1864, 1873, 1874, 1875, 1876, 1877, 1880, 1884, and 1886]

(In Thorpe, Francis Newton, comp. The federal and state constitutions, colonial charters, and other organic laws of the states, territories, and colonies now or heretofore forming the United States of America. Washington, 1909. v. 1, p. 547-554)

[Ct 7]
Connecticut. Constitution.
The constitution of Connecticut, including all amendments to date and excluding such parts as are not now in force, being the constitution as it now exists in legal effect and with its original language and arrangement. Also the Constitution of the United

[Ct 7, cont.]
States reprinted in full from the revised statutes of the United
States . . . Hartford, 1901.
   44 p.

   Constitution of the United States: p. 25-44.

[Ct 8]
Connecticut. Constitutional Convention, 1902.
   [Miscellaneous documents. Hartford, 1902]
   1 v. (various pagings)

   Contents.—Roll of delegates to the constitutional convention of
Connecticut.—Proposed constitution of Connecticut to be submitted to the electors for adoption or rejection, June 16, 1902.—
The debate on constitutional amendments. Session 1901. Mr.
James G. Batterson and Ex.-Gov. Morgan G. Bulkeley. (Includes
text of the bill presented to the 1901 General Assembly calling
a constitutional convention)—Constitutional convention of
Connecticut, 1902, by J. M. Berry.—Proposed amendment to
the constitution (1899?)—The power station of machine politics, by L. E. Whiton.—"By the holy crowbar"—Roll of the convention.—The following facts are furnished in explanation of the
plan of representation, etc.—The reason why.—Increasing representation, who are to get it?

[Ct 9]
Connecticut. Constitutional Convention, 1902.
   Journal of the constitutional convention of Connecticut, 1902.
Hartford, 1902.
   493 p.

   Constitution, as adopted, p. 444-467.

[Ct 10]
Connecticut. Constitutional Convention, 1902.
   Rules and orders of the constitutional convention of Connecticut, 1902. [Hartford] 1902.
   8 p.

[Ct 11]
Connecticut. Constitutional Convention, 1902.
[Documents 1-4. Hartford?] 1902.
1 v. (various pagings)

Contents.— 1. Representation in Senate and House of Representatives; extracts from the constitution of Rhode Island.—
2. Creation of corporations; from New York annotated constitution, 1894.—3. Private and local bills not to be passed in certain
cases; from New York annotated constitution, 1894.—4. No
member to receive an appointment; from New York annotated
constitution, 1894.

[Ct 12]
Connecticut. Constitution.
Article of amendment to the constitution [ratified 1905]

(In Thorpe, Francis Newton, comp. The federal and state constitutions, colonial charters, and other organic laws of the states,
territories, and colonies now or heretofore forming the United
States of America. Washington, 1909. v. 1, p. 555)

[Ct 13]
Connecticut. Constitution.
Proposed amendment to the constitution in the form of a revision of the constitution. [Hartford, 1907]
12 p.

[Ct 14]
Connecticut. Constitution.
The constitution of Connecticut.

(In Connecticut. Secretary of state. Register and manual of the
state of Connecticut, 1960. Hartford, 1960. p. 36-50)

Delaware

[De 3, cont.]
altering, and amending the constitution of this state, or if they
see occasion, for forming a new one instead thereof. Wilmington
[1792]
  107 p.

[De 4]
Delaware. Constitutional Convention, 1791-1792.
  Minutes of the Grand Committee of the Whole Convention of
the Delaware State, which commenced at Dover, on Tuesday, the
twenty-ninth day of November, in the year of our Lord one thousand seven hundred and ninety-one, for the purpose of reviewing,
altering, and amending the constitution of this state, or, if they
see occasion, for forming a new one instead thereof. Wilmington,
1792.
  80 p.

[De 5]
Delaware. Constitution.
  Constitution of Delaware—1792.

  (In Thorpe, Francis Newton, comp. The federal and state constitutions, colonial charters, and other organic laws of the states,
territories, and colonies now or heretofore forming the United
States of America. Washington, 1909. v. 1, p. 568-581)

[De 6]
Delaware. Constitutional Convention, 1831.
  Journal of the convention of the people of the state of Delaware,
which assembled at Dover, in the year of our Lord, one thousand
eight hundred and thirty-one, and of the independence of the
United States, the fifty-sixth. Wilmington [1832?]
  129, [1] p.

  Amended constitution: p. 81-99.

[De 7]
Delaware. Constitutional Convention, 1831.
    Journal in Committee of the Whole of the convention of the
people of the state of Delaware, which assembled at Dover, in the
year 1831, and of the independence of the United States the
fifty-sixth. Wilmington [1832?]
    42 p.

[De 8]
Delaware. Constitutional Convention, 1831.
    Debates of the Delaware convention, for revising the constitu-
tion of the state, or adopting a new one; held at Dover, November,
1831. (Reported for the Delaware Gazette and American Watch-
man) by William M. Gouge. Wilmington, 1831.
    264, [3] p.

    "The amended Constitution of the State of Delaware":
p. [245]-264.

[De 9]
Delaware. Constitutional Convention, 1852-1853.
    Journal of the convention of the people of the state of Dela-
ware . . . at Dover . . . 1852 and . . . 1853. Wilmington, 1853.
    216 p.

[De 10]
Delaware. Constitutional Convention, 1852-1853.
    Journal in Committee of the Whole, of the convention of the
people of the state of Delaware, assembled at Dover, by their
delegates, December seventh and eighth 1852, and afterwards,
by adjournment, from March 10 to April 30, 1853, inclusive.
Wilmington, 1853.
    60 p.

[De 11]
Delaware. Constitutional Convention, 1852-1853.
    Debates and proceedings of the constitutional convention of the
state of Delaware. Reported by Richard Sutton, Esq., stenographer

[De 11, cont.]
to the U. S. Senate, together with the amended constitution and schedule, and a tabular statement showing the names, ages, occupations, etc., of the members of the convention. Dover, 1853.
317, [2] p.

[De 12]
Delaware. Constitution.
Amendments to the constitution of 1831.

(In Thorpe, Francis Newton, comp. The federal and state constitutions, colonial charters, and other organic laws of the states, territories, and colonies now or heretofore forming the United States of America. Washington, 1909, v. 1, p. 600)

[De 13]
Delaware. Constitutional Convention, 1896-1897.
Journal of the constitutional convention of the state of Delaware, convened and held at Dover, on Tuesday, the first day of December, A. D. 1896 . . . Georgetown, 1897.
580, 42 p.

Constitution: p. 523-577.

[De 14]
Delaware. Constitutional Convention, 1896-1897.
Journal of Committee of the Whole of the constitutional convention of the state of Delaware, convened and held at Dover, on Tuesday, the first day of December, A. D. 1896 . . . Dover, 1897.
391, 40 p.

[De 15]
Delaware. Constitutional Convention, 1896-1897.
Debates and proceedings . . . reported by Charles G. Guyer and Edmond C. Hardesty, stenographers to the United States courts and courts of Delaware; commencing December 1, 1896, Dover, Delaware. [Dover?] 1958.
5 v. (3564 p.)

[De 16]
Delaware. Constitutional Convention, 1896-1897.
Manual of the constitutional convention, containing the officers, members, standing and special committees and the rules. [Dover, 1896]
18 p.

[De 17]
Delaware. Constitution.
Constitution of the state of Delaware, as adopted in convention, June 4, 1897, with amendments made subsequently thereto. [Dover] 1964.
60, 27 p.

Florida

[Fl 1]
Florida. Constitutional Convention, 1838-1839.
Journal of the proceedings of a convention of delegates to form a constitution for the people of Florida, held at St. Joseph, December, 1838. St. Joseph, 1839.
120 p.

Convention met December 3, 1838; adjourned January 11, 1839.

——. Constitution or form of government, for the people of Florida. [St. Joseph, 1839]
20 p.

[Fl 2]
Florida. Constitution.
Constitution or form of government, for the people of Florida. By authority: published under the direction of the secretary of state. Tallahassee, 1851.
27, iii p.

"Amendments to the Constitution . . .: adopted 1846-1850": p. [25]-27, i-iii.

[Fl 3]
Florida. Convention, 1861-1862.
Journal of the proceedings of the convention of the people of

[Fl 3, cont.]
Florida, begun and held at the Capitol in the city of Tallahassee,
on Thursday, January 3, A. D. 1861. Tallahassee, 1861; reprinted,
Jacksonville, 1928.
    124, 77 p.

    "Ordinances & resolutions passed by the State Convention . . .
begun . . . January 3, 1861": p. [109]-124, and "Proceedings of
the Convention of the people of Florida, at called sessions, begun . . . February 26, and . . . April 18, 1861": 77 p. at end, have
half-title pages.

[Fl 4]
Florida. Convention, 1861-1862.
    Journal of the convention of the people of Florida, at called
session, begun and held at the Capitol, in the city of Tallahassee,
on Tuesday, January 14, 1862. [Tallahassee, 1862]
    110 p.

    Adjourned January 27, 1862.
    Page 94 incorrectly numbered 64.

[Fl 5]
Florida. Constitution.
    Constitution or form of government for the people . . . as re-
vised and amended at a convention of the people begun and
holden at the city of Tallahassee on the 3d day of January, A. D.
1861, and at a called session thereof begun and held January 14,
A. D. 1862, with the ordinances adopted by said convention at
said called session. Tallahassee, 1861.
    48 p.

[Fl 6]
Florida. Constitutional Convention, 1865.
    Journal of proceedings of the convention of Florida, begun and
held at the Capitol of the state, at Tallahassee, Wednesday, October 25, A. D. 1865. Tallahassee, 1865.
    167 p.

[Fl 6, cont.]

"Constitution or form of government for the people of Florida": p. [135]-158.

[Fl 7]
Florida. Constitutional Convention, 1868.

Journal of the proceedings of the constitutional convention of the state of Florida, begun and held at the Capitol, at Tallahassee, on Monday, January 20, 1868. Tallahassee, 1868.

134 p.

[Fl 8]
Florida. Constitutional Convention, 1868.

Proceedings of the Florida convention . . . [Washington, 1868] 31 p. ([U. S.] 40th Cong. 2d sess. House. Misc. Doc. 114)

Ordered printed March 31, 1868.
Signed: Wm. H. Gleason, George J. Alden.
"Constitution of the State of Florida": p. 11-31.

Caption title.

[Fl 9]
Florida. Constitution.

Constitution of the state of Florida, framed at a convention of the people, begun and held at the city of Tallahassee, on the 20th day of January, A. D., 1868. Together with the ordinances adopted by said convention. Published in compliance with a resolution of said convention, by Sherman Conant, secretary of the convention. Jacksonville, 1868.

42 p.

[Fl 10]
Florida. Constitution.

Constitution of the state of Florida, with notes of the decisions and opinions of the Supreme Court, up to and including January term, 1877. Tallahassee, 1877.

Caption title: Constitution of the state of Florida, as amended in 1871 and 1875.

[Fl 11]
Florida. Constitutional Convention, 1885.
Journal of the proceedings of the constitutional convention of
the state of Florida, which convened at the Capitol, at Tallahassee,
on Tuesday, June 9, 1885 . . . Tallahassee, 1885.
631 p.

"Constitution adopted by the Convention of 1885": p. [589] -
627.

[Fl 12]
Thursby, Vincent V.
Index to the journal of the proceedings of the constitutional
convention of the state of Florida, 1885, by Vincent V. Thursby
. . . and Annie Mary Hartsfield . . . Tallahassee, 1965.
ix, 45 p.

[Fl 13]
Florida. Constitution.
Constitution of the state of Florida adopted by the convention
of 1885 (as amended) [Tallahassee] 1954.
119 p.

"Ordinances of the Constitutional Convention of 1885": p. 3-6.
Constitutional amendments adopted at 1954 general election,
1 l., laid in.

[Fl 14]
Florida. Constitution Advisory Commission.
[Research reports. Gainesville, 1955?]
1 v. (various pagings)

Ernest R. Bartley, director of research.
Research reports nos. 2-16 bound in one volume; no. 1, now out
of print, is not a report, but consists of the assignment of articles
of the constitution to the committees.

[Fl 15]
Florida. Constitution Advisory Commission.
Recommended constitution for Florida. [Ocala, 1957]
iv, 55, xxxi p.

Index prepared by the Statutory Revision Dept., Office of the
Attorney General.

[Fl 16]
Florida. Constitution Advisory Commission.
Handbook on recommended constitution for Florida. [Talla-
hassee? 1957]
96 p.

"Designed to implement the text of the recommended constitution for Florida, submitted to the Legislature."

[Fl 17]
Florida. Legislature.
Revised Florida constitution proposed by the legislature, and
explanation of changes. Tallahassee [1957?]
41 p.

Cover title.
"Commentary": 1 l. inserted.
Analysis prepared by Dr. George John Miller and Douglas B.
Shivers, attorneys for the legislative committees on constitutional
revision.

[Fl 18]
Florida. Constitution.
Constitution of the state of Florida adopted by the convention of
1885 (as amended —— 1958) [Tallahassee] 1958.

[Fl 19]
Bain, Richard E.
The proposed Florida constitution of 1958 and the constitution
of 1885: a comparison. Tallahassee, 1958.

[Fl 19, cont.]

49 p. (Florida. State University. School of Public Administration. Bureau of Government Research and Service. Studies in Government, no. 23)

[Fl 20]
Florida. Legislature. Senate.

A joint resolution proposing revision of the . . . constitution of the state of Florida. [Tallahassee? 1959?]

1 v. (various pagings)

Caption title.

[Fl 21]
Florida. Special Constitution Advisory Committee to the
    Governor.

The 1959 recommended constitution. [Tallahassee? 1959?]
1 v. (various pagings)

No title page.
"Work done by the Statutory Revision Department [of the Attorney General's Office] and the Special Constitution Advisory Committee to the Governor."

[Fl 22]
Florida. Constitution.

Constitution of the state of Florida adopted by convention of 1885, as amended.

(In Florida. Laws, statutes, etc. Florida statutes, 1959. [c1959] v. 3, p. 3379-3419)

Georgia

[Ga 1]
Georgia. Constitution.
The constitution of the state of Georgia. Savannah, 1785.
21 p.

In convention, January 24, 1777.
There are no known official records extant of the convention
which met in Savannah from October 1, 1776, to February 5,
1777, and agreed upon this constitution. Cf. F. M. Green. Constitutional development in the South Atlantic states, 1776-1860.
1930.

[Ga 2]
Georgia. Constitution.
The constitution of the state of Georgia. Ratified the 6th of
May, 1789. Augusta, 1789.
24 p.

Framed by a convention which met in Augusta on November
4-24, 1788. Amended and ratified by another convention, chosen
for that purpose, which met in Augusta January 4 to May 6, 1789.

[Ga 3]
Georgia. Constitutional Convention, 1795.
Journal of the convention of the state of Georgia, convened at
Louisville, on Monday, May 3, 1795, for the purpose of taking into

[Ga 3, cont.]
consideration, the alterations necessary to be made in the existing
constitution of this state. To which are added, their amendments
to the constitution. Augusta, 1795.
    32 p.

[Ga 4]
Georgia. Constitutional Convention, 1798.
    Journal of the convention of the state of Georgia. [Louisville?
1798?]
    28 p.

    Caption title.

[Ga 5]
Georgia. Constitution.
    Constitution of Georgia — 1798.

    (In Thorpe, Francis Newton, comp. The federal and state con-
stitutions, colonial charters, and other organic laws of the states,
territories, and colonies now or heretofore forming the United
States of America. Washington, 1909. v. 2, p. 791-802)

[Ga 6]
Georgia. Constitution.
    Amendments to the constitution of 1798 [ratified 1808, 1812,
1818, 1819, and 1824]

    (In Thorpe, Francis Newton, comp. The federal and state con-
stitutions, colonial charters and other organic laws of the states,
territories, and colonies now or heretofore forming the United
States of America. Washington, 1909. v. 2, p. 802-805)

[Ga 8]
Georgia. Convention, 1833.
    Journal of a general convention of the state of Georgia, to
reduce the members of the General Assembly. Begun and held
at Milledgeville, the seat of government, in May, 1833. Milledgeville, 1833.
    56 p.

[Ga 9]
Georgia. Constitution.
Amendments to the constitution of 1798 [ratified 1833 and 1835]

(In Thorpe, Francis Newton, comp. The federal and state constitutions, colonial charters, and other organic laws of the states, territories, and colonies now or heretofore forming the United States of America. Washington, 1909. v. 2, p. 805-807)

[Ga 10]
Georgia. Convention, 1839.
Journal of the convention, to reduce and equalize the representation of the General Assembly of the state of Georgia, assembled in Milledgeville, on the 6th day of May, eighteen hundred and thirty-nine. Milledgeville, 1839.
74 p.

[Ga 11]
Georgia. Constitution.
Amendments to the constitution of 1798 [ratified 1840, 1841, 1843, 1847, and 1849]

(In Thorpe, Francis Newton, comp. The federal and state constitutions, colonial charters, and other organic laws of the states, territories, and colonies now or heretofore forming the United States of America. Washington, 1909. v. 2, p. 807-809)

[Ga 12]
Georgia. Convention, 1861.
Journal of the public and secret proceedings of the convention of the people of Georgia, held in Milledgeville [January 16-25] and Savannah [March 7-23] in 1861. Together with the ordinances adopted. Milledgeville, 1861.
416 p.

Revised constitution: p. 285-300.

[Ga 13]
Georgia. Convention, 1865.
Journal of the proceedings of the convention of the people of Georgia, held in Milledgeville in October and November, 1865; together with the ordinances and resolutions adopted. Milledgeville, 1865.
269 p.
The constitution of the state of Georgia: p. 207-226.

[Ga 14]
Georgia. Constitutional Convention, 1867-1868.
Journal of the proceedings of the constitutional convention of the people of Georgia, held in the city of Atlanta in the months of December, 1867, and January, February, and March, 1868. And ordinances and resolutions adopted. Augusta, 1868.
636 p.

[Ga 15]
Georgia. Constitution.
Constitution, ordinances and resolutions of the Georgia convention, assembled in pursuance of the reconstruction acts of Congress, and held, by order of General Pope, in the city of Atlanta, in 1867 and 1868 . . . Atlanta, 1868.
47 p.

[Ga 16]
Georgia. Constitution.
The constitution of the state of Georgia, with full marginal notes and a copious and analytical index thereto. By John L. Conley. [n. p.] 1870.
88 p.

[Ga 17]
Georgia. Constitutional Convention, 1877.
Journal of the constitutional convention of the people of Georgia, held in the city of Atlanta in the months of July and August, 1877. Atlanta, 1877.
[7]-701 p.
"Constitution of the State of Georgia – 1877": p. [573]-631.

[Ga 18]
Georgia. Constitutional Convention, 1877.
A stenographic report of the proceedings of the constitutional convention held in Atlanta, Georgia, 1877. Giving debates in full on all questions before the convention. Reported by Samuel W. Small for the Atlanta Constitution. Atlanta, 1877.
502 p.

[Ga 19]
Georgia. Constitution.
The constitution of Georgia, as adopted December 5, 1877, with a copious analytical index and full marginal notes. Prepared by Thos. J. Chappell and Henry R. Goetchius . . . Columbus, 1879.
79 p.

[Ga 20]
Georgia. Constitution.
Constitution of the state of Georgia of 1877, as amended through 1943. Compiled by T. Grady Head . . . Assisted by Marshall L. Allison . . . [and others]. Appendix showing proposals to amend the constitution prepared by Ella May Thornton. [Atlanta, 1943]
155 p.

With appendix of amendments submitted, act creating constitutional commission, Commission to Revise Constitution, cross-references, and editorial notes.

[Ga 21]
Georgia. State Commission to Revise the Constitution.
Records. Edited by Albert B. Saye. [Atlanta] 1946.
2 v.

"Revised Constitution": v. 2, p. 547-615.

[Ga 22]
Georgia. State Commission to Revise the Constitution.
Report and recommendations of sub-committee no. 1[-7] to

[Ga 22, cont.]
State Commission to Revise the Constitution. [Atlanta] 1944.
1 v. (various pagings)

[Ga 23]
Georgia. Constitution.
Proposed new constitution of the state of Georgia, as adopted by the General Assembly session of 1945. [Atlanta, 1945]
93 p., facsim.

On cover: To be submitted to the voters of Georgia at the general election to be held August 7, 1945.

[Ga 24]
U. S. Constitution.
Constitutions of the United States and of the state of Georgia; with amendments to date, annotated. Comp. and annotated by Harry B. Skillman and Harry S. Strozier. Atlanta [1948]
676, 53 p.

[Ga 25]
Georgia. University. Institute of Government.
Table of amendments of the constitution of Georgia, 1945-1966. Edited by Albert B. Saye. [Athens] 1967.
[3], 40 numb. l.

Originally prepared in 1963 primarily for use by the Constitutional Revision Commission. Updated to include amendments voted on in 1964 and 1966.

Hawaii

[Ha 4]
—— . Subject index to Hawaii constitutional convention topics
. . . [Honolulu, 1968]
 1 p. l., 35 numb. l., tables.

[Ha 5]
Hawaii. Constitution.
 The constitution of the state of Hawaii, agreed upon by the
delegates of the people of Hawaii in convention, at Iolani Palace,
Honolulu . . . on July 22, 1950. [Honolulu, 1959]
 32 p.

[Ha 6]
—— . Index to the constitution . . . [Prepared by the Legislative
Reference Bureau, August 25, 1959. Honolulu, 1959]
 10 numb. l.

Idaho

[Id 1]
Idaho (Ter.) Constitutional Convention, 1889.
   Proceedings and debates of the constitutional convention of Idaho, 1889, edited and annotated by I. W. Hart . . . Caldwell, 1912.
   2 v. (x, 2143 p.)

[Id 2]
Idaho. Constitution.
   Constitution of the state of Idaho. Adopted in convention at Boise City, August 6, 1889. Boise City, 1889.
   42 p.

   Cover title.
   Also published in (U. S.) 51st Cong. 1st sess. Senate. Misc. Doc. 39.

[Id 3]
Idaho. Constitution.
   Constitution of the state of Idaho, with all amendments. Revised 1949. [Boise, 1949]
   68 p.

[Id 4]
Idaho. Constitution.

Constitution of the state of Idaho. Includes amendments approved at the 1956 general election. Published by Jas. H. Young, secretary of state. Boise, 1958.

58 p.

Illinois

[Il 1]
Illinois. Constitutional Convention, 1818.
    Journal of the convention [begun and held at the town of
Kaskaskia on Monday the third day of August, 1818].
    72 p., map

    (In Illinois State Historical Society. Journal. v. 6, no. 3,
October, 1913, p. 355-424)

[Il 2]
Illinois. Constitution.
    The constitution of the state of Illinois, adopted in convention,
at Kaskaskia, on the twenty-sixth day of August, in the year of
our Lord one thousand eight hundred and eighteen, and of the
independence of the United States, the forty-third. Kaskaskia,
1818.
    24 p.

[Il 3]
Illinois. Constitutional Convention, 1874.
    Journal of the convention, assembled at Springfield, June 7,
1847, in pursuance of an act of the General Assembly of the
state of Illinois . . . approved, February 20, 1847, for the purpose of altering, amending, or revising the constitution of . . .

[Il 3, cont.]
Illinois. Published by authority of the convention. Springfield, 1847.

  592 p.

  Constitution: p. 544-572.

[Il 4]
Illinois. Constitutional Convention, 1847.
  The constitutional debates of 1847. Edited with introduction and notes by Arthur Charles Cole. Springfield, 1919.

  4 p. l., iii-xxx, 1018 p. (Collections of the Illinois State Historical Library, v. xiv. Constitutional series, v. 11)

  Bibliography: p. 987-995.

[Il 5]
Illinois. Constitution.
  Constitution of the state of Illinois, adopted by the convention, assembled at Springfield, June 7, 1847, in pursuance of an act of the General Assembly of the state of Illinois, entitled "An act to provide for the call of a convention." Published by order of the convention. Springfield, 1847.

  39 p.

  At head of title: Illinois constitutional convention.
  "Address to the people of Illinois. August 30, 1847. Adopted by the convention, and ordered to be printed with the constitution published for distribution": p. 33-39.

[Il 6]
Illinois. Constitutional Convention, 1862.
  Journal of the constitutional convention of the state of Illinois, convened at Springfield, January 7, 1862. Springfield, 1862.

  1131, xv p.

  "New constitution of the State of Illinois": p. 1072-1114.
  The constitution framed by this convention was rejected by vote of the people.

[Il 7]
Illinois. Constitution.
New constitution of the state of Illinois, adopted by the constitutional convention at Springfield, March 24, 1862, and submitted to the people for ratification or rejection, at an election to be held June 17, 1862. With an address to the people of Illinois. Springfield, 1862.
56 p.
At head of title: Illinois constitutional convention.
This constitution was rejected by vote of the people.

[Il 8]
Illinois. Constitutional Convention, 1869-1870.
Journal of the constitutional convention of the state of Illinois. Convened at Springfield, December 13, 1869. Springfield, 1870.
1022 p., 1 l., xi p., 4 l.
Opposite pages 198, 588, 622, and 669 are pages "set apart" in memory of deceased members of the convention.
"Constitution of the state of Illinois": p. 993-1019.

[Il 9]
Illinois. Constitutional Convention, 1869-1870.
Debates and proceedings of the constitutional convention of the state of Illinois, convened at the city of Springfield, Tuesday, December 13, 1869. Ely, Burnham & Bartlett, official stenographers . . . Springfield, 1870.
2 v. (1895, [1], 132 p.)

Partial contents of v. 2:—Constitution adopted in 1870. p. 1871-1880.—Constitution adopted in 1848. p. [1881]-1888.—Constitution adopted in 1818. p. [1889]-1892.—An act to provide for calling a convention to revise, alter or amend the constitution of the state of Illinois, approved February 25, 1869. p. [1893]—Abstract of the vote cast for and against the adoption of the new constitution, and for and against the articles submitted therewith. p. 1894-1895.—Proclamation. p. [1896]—Index to the debates and proceedings of the Illinois constitutional convention of 1870. 132 p. at end.

[Il 10]
Illinois. Constitutional Convention, 1869-1870.
Manual for the constitutional convention of the state of Illinois. 1869-1870. Constitutions. Chicago, 1869.
iv, 476 p.

[Il 11]
Illinois. Constitution.
The constitution of the state of Illinois, as adopted in convention, May 13, 1870, and submitted to the people for adoption or rejection at an election to be held July 2, A. D. 1870, and the address of the convention accompanying the same. Springfield, 1870.
49, 10 p.

Cover title.

[Il 12]
Illinois. Constitution.
Constitution of the state of Illinois, annotated. Compiled and published by the Legislative Reference Bureau. Printed by authority of the state of Illinois. [Springfield, 1919]
319 p.

At head of title: Constitutional convention.
Ratified by the people, July 2, 1870. In force, August 8, 1870. Amendments were adopted in 1878, 1880, 1884, 1886, 1890, 1904, and 1908.

[Il 13]
Illinois. Legislative Reference Bureau.
List of suggestions for constitutional change together with texts of constitutions of Illinois. Compiled and published by the Legislative Reference Bureau. Printed by authority of the state of Illinois. [Springfield, 1919]
183 p.

At head of title: Constitutional convention.

[Il 14]
Illinois. Constitutional Convention, 1920-1922.

Journal of the constitutional convention, 1920-1922, of the state of Illinois. Convened at the Capitol in Springfield, January 6, 1920, and adjourned sine die October 10, 1922. Printed by authority of the state of Illinois. [Springfield, 1922]

974 p.

[Il 15]
Illinois. Constitutional Convention, 1920-1922.

Journal of the Committee of the Whole of the Constitutional Convention, 1920-1922, of the state of Illinois. Convened at the Capitol in Springfield, January 6, 1920, and adjourned sine die October 10, 1922. Printed by authority of the state of Illinois. [Springfield, 1922]

227 p.

[Il 16]
Illinois. Constitutional Convention, 1920-1922.

Proceedings of the constitutional convention of the state of Illinois convened January 6, 1920 . . . Compiled by Committee to Edit the Proceedings of the Convention . . . Printed by authority of the state of Illinois. [Springfield, 1922]

5 v. (4938 p.)

William S. Gray, John L. Dryer, Rodney H. Brandom, Committee to Edit the Proceedings of the Convention.

Partial contents of v. 1:—Constitutional convention (Senate joint resolution no. 1) . . . p. 4—Official proclamation. p. 5—Act calling constitutional convention. p. 6-8.—List of delegates. p. 9-10—List of delegates by districts. p. 11-17.—Summary of delegates of the constitutional convention. p. 18.—Rules of the constitutional convention. p. 19-26.—Committees. p. 27-28.—Committee assignments by delegates. p. 29-32.

Running title: Debates of the constitutional convention.

[Il 18]
Illinois. Constitutional Convention, 1920-1922.
Reports nos. 1 to 19 of the Committee on Phraseology and
Style . . . Formal parts omitted. [Springfield, 1922]
196 p.

[Il 19]
Illinois. Constitutional Convention, 1920-1922.
Delegates' manual of the fifth constitutional convention of the
state of Illinois, 1920. Including data relative to the calling and
assembling of the convention, together with a list of delegates,
rules, committees, portraits, biographies and other information
concerning the organization and work of the convention. Edited
by B. H. McCann, secretary. [Springfield, 1920]
256 p. incl. ports., tables, charts, fold. plan.

[Il 20]
Illinois. Legislative Reference Bureau.
Constitutional convention bulletins. Compiled and published by
the Legislative Reference Bureau, Springfield, Illinois. Printed by
authority of the state of Illinois. [Springfield, 1920]
xxxiii, [3]-1224 p., fold. charts, tables (part fold.)

Includes fifteen bulletins, each with special title page.

[Il 21]
Illinois. Legislative Reference Bureau.
General statement of work of Legislative Reference Bureau and
a consolidated index to constitutional convention bulletins no. 1-
15. Printed by authority of the state of Illinois. [Springfield,
1919]
20 p.

At head of title: Constitutional convention.

[Il 22]
Illinois. Constitution.
The proposed new constitution of Illinois, 1922. With explana-
tory notes and address to the people. For submission to the peo-

[Il 22, cont.]
ple at a special election on Tuesday, December 12, 1922. Illinois
constitutional convention, 1920-1922. Printed by authority of
the state of Illinois. [Chicago, 1922]
    80 p.

[Il 23]
**Illinois. General Assembly. Special Committee on Constitutional
    Amendment.**
    Explanation and arguments on the proposed amendment to
section 2, article XIV of the constitution of the state of Illinois.
To be submitted to the voters at the general election to be held
November 4, 1924. Louis L. Emmerson, secretary of state.
Printed by authority of the state of Illinois. [Springfield, 1924]
    6 p.

    Report of Special Committee on Constitutional Amendment,
June 30, 1923, signed: K. C. Ronalds, J. W. Rausch, Thomas J.
Hair, committee on the part of the House of Representatives;
Epler C. Mills, Thurlow G. Essington, committee on the part of
the Senate.

[Il 24]
Illinois. Legislative Council. Research Dept.
    Constitutional revision in Illinois; report pursuant to proposal
243 sponsored by Representative Bernice T. Van der Vries . . .
Springfield [1947]
    [2] l., ii, 41 numb. l. incl. tables. (Its Publication, no. 85.
December, 1957)

    Cover title.

[Il 25]
Illinois. Judicial Article Revision Commission.
    Report submitted April 14, 1953. Springfield [1953]
    28 p.

    "Pursuant to Senate Bill 397 of the 67th General Assembly."

[Il 26]
Illinois. Constitution.

Constitution of the state of Illinois, adopted May 13, 1870 [as amended 1954] Issued by . . . secretary of state. [Springfield, 1955]

86 p.

[Il 27]
Illinois. Constitution.

Amendment to the constitution of Illinois (revenue amendment) that will be submitted to the voters November 6, 1956. Amends sections 1, 2, 3, 9, and 10 of article IX and repeals section 13 of article IX. Published in compliance with statute by Charles F. Carpentier, secretary of state. [Springfield, 1956]

6 p.

[Il 28]
Illinois. Legislative Council.

Legislative documents dealing with the proposed constitutional amendments. To be submitted at the general election, November 4, 1958. [n. p., 1957]

1 p. l., i, 13 p.

Caption title.

[Il 29]
Illinois. Constitution.

Text and explanatory summary of the proposed judicial article. [Springfield, 1958?]

12 p.

Proposed judicial article to supersede present article VI of the state constitutions, to be submitted to the voters at the general election in November, 1958.

[Il 30]

Illinois. Committee for Constitutional Revision. Committee for
     Modern Courts.

Fact-book for the blue ballot judicial amendment . . . Chicago
[1958]
     35 p.

Cover title.

[Il 31]
Illinois. Constitution.

Constitution of the state of Illinois. Adopted May 13, 1870.
Issued by Charles F. Carpentier [secretary of state. Springfield,
1961]
     87 p.

"Constitution of the United States": p. 68-87.

Indiana

[In 3, cont.]

dence of the United States, the fortieth.

(In Indiana. Laws, statutes, etc. The revised laws of Indiana
. . . 1824. p. 34-54)

[In 4]

Indiana. Constitutional Convention, 1850-1851.

Journal of the convention of the people of the state of Indiana,
to amend the constitution. Assembled at Indianapolis, October,
1850. Indianapolis, 1851.

1085 p.

[In 5]

Indiana. Constitutional Convention, 1850-1851.

Report of the debates and proceedings of the convention for
the revision of the constitution of the state of Indiana. 1850.
H. Fowler, official reporter to the convention . . . Indianapolis,
1850-[1851]

2 v. (2107 p.)

Convention met October 7, 1850; adjourned February 10,
1851.

Constitution: v. 2, p. 2066-2077.

[In 6]

Indiana. Constitutional Convention, 1850-1851.

Index to the journal and debates of the Indiana constitutional
convention, 1850-1851. Compiled by Jessie P. Boswell. Published by the Indiana Historical Bureau, Indianapolis. [Indian-
apolis] 1938.

136 p.

[In 7]

Indiana. Constitution.

Constitution of the state of Indiana, and the address of the

[In 7, cont.]
constitutional convention. New Albany, Ind., 1851.
   32 p.
   Cover title.

[In 8]
Dunn, Jacob Platt.
   The proposed constitution of Indiana. Indianapolis, 1911.
   47, 8 p.

   "Addendum: The Indiana Constitution. Parallel columns showing proposed changes. To be voted on in November, 1912": 8 p.
at end.

[In 9]
Conference on the Question "Shall a Constitutional Convention
      be called in Indiana?"
   Proceedings of a conference on the question "Shall a constitutional convention be called in Indiana?" Held at Indiana University, Bloomington, Indiana, Monday, Tuesday, and Wednesday, June 8, 9, and 10, 1914. [Bloomington, 1914]
   250 p. (Indiana University Bulletin, v. XII, no. 12, November, 1914)

   At head of title: Indiana University. Extension Division.

[In 10]
Indiana. Constitution.
   Constitution of the state of Indiana, edited and annotated by
the Legislative Bureau. November, 1957. [Indianapolis, 1957]
   36 p.

Iowa

[Ia 1]
Iowa. Constitutional Convention, 1844.
Propositions for a constitutional convention.

(In Iowa. State Historical Society. Documentary material relating to the history of Iowa [1895-1901] v. 1, p. 133-149)

[Ia 2]
Iowa. Constitutional Convention, 1844.
Journal of the convention for the formation of a constitution
for the state of Iowa, begun and held at Iowa City, on the first
Monday of October, eighteen hundred and forty-four. Published
by authority. Iowa City, 1845.
224 p.

Bound with Iowa. Constitutional convention, 1846. Journal . . .
Iowa City, 1846.

[Ia 3]
Iowa. Constitution.
The constitution of 1844.

(In Iowa. State Historical Society. Documentary material relating to the history of Iowa [1895-1901] v. 1, p. 150-174)

[Ia 4]
Iowa. Constitutional Convention, 1846.
    Journal of the convention for the formation of a constitution
for the state of Iowa, begun and held at Iowa City, on the first
Monday of May, eighteen hundred and forty-six. Iowa City, 1846.
    xxi, [23]-120 p. [With Iowa. Constitutional convention, 1844.
Journal . . . Iowa City, 1845]

    "The Constitution": p. [iii]-xxi.

[Ia 5]
Shambaugh, Benjamin Franklin, ed.
    Fragments of the debates of the Iowa constitutional conven-
tions of 1844 and 1846, along with press comments and other
materials on the constitutions of 1844 and 1846. Iowa City, 1900.
    iv p., 1 l., 415 p.

[Ia 6]
Iowa. Constitution.
    The constitution of 1846.

    (In Iowa. State Historical Society. Documentary material relat-
ing to the history of Iowa [1895-1901] v. 1, p. 190-211)

[Ia 7]
Iowa. Constitutional Convention, 1857.
    Journal of the constitutional convention of the state of Iowa,
in session at Iowa City, from the nineteenth day of January, A. D.,
one thousand eight hundred and fifty-seven, to the fifth day of
March of the same year inclusive. Muscatine, 1857.
    406, 26 p.

    "Constitution of the State of Iowa": 26 p. at end of volume.

[Ia 8]
Iowa. Constitutional Convention, 1857.
    The debates of the constitutional convention of the state of
Iowa, assembled at Iowa City, Monday, January 19, 1857. Being
a full . . . report of the debates and proceedings, by authority of

[Ia 8, cont.]
the convention, accompanied . . . by a copious index of subjects, and remarks of members thereon. Official. W. Blair Lord, reporter . . . Davenport, 1857.

2 v.

"Old and new constitutions" in parallel columns." v. 2, p. [1067]-1096.

[Ia 9]
Iowa. Constitution.
Constitution of the state of Iowa, with judicial constructions and interpretations by state and federal courts.

(Iowa. Laws, statutes, etc. Iowa code annotated. St. Paul [1949-1951] v. 1-2)

Kansas

[Kan 1]
Kansas (Ter.) Delegate Convention, 1855.
Proceedings of the territorial delegate convention, held at Big Springs, on 5-6 of September, 1855. Lawrence [1855]
16 p.

"Proceedings of the State Constitutional Convention, held at Topeka, Kansas T., September 19-20, 1855": p. [9]-12.
"People's proclamation." Signed: By order of the Executive Committee of Kansas Territory. J. H. Lane, chairman. J. K. Goodin, secretary: p. 14-16.

[Kan 2]
U. S. Congress. House. Committee on the Territories.
. . . Memorial of the senators and representatives, and the constitution of the state of Kansas; also, the majority and minority reports of the Committee on Territories on the said constitution. Washington, 1856.

[Kan 3]
Kansas (Ter.) Constitutional Convention, 1857.
[Journal]

(In [U. S.] Cong. House. Select Committee of Fifteen. Kansas constitution. [Washington? 1858?] p. 22-73)

No title page.

[Kan 4]
Kansas (Ter.) Legislature.
   Report of the president of the council and speaker of the House
of Representatives of the territory of Kansas, on the result of the
vote of December 21, for the Lecompton Constitution, and on the
result of the election of January 4 under said constitution; also
proclamation of the acting governor, the president of the council,
and the speaker of the House of Representatives, on the result
of the vote of January 4 on the submission of the Lecompton
Constitution to a vote of the people. [n. p., 1858?]
   Broadside.

[Kan 5]
U. S. President, 1857-1861 (Buchanan)
   Message of the President of the United States, communicating a
constitution for Kansas as a state, and presenting his views in relation to the affairs of that territory, February 2, 1858. Read. Mo-
tion of Mr. Bigler to print and refer to the Committee on Territories debated. Adjourned, February 3, 1858. Ordered to be
printed, with constitution and papers. [Washington, 1858]
   32 p. [(U. S.] 35th Cong., 1st sess. Senate. Ex. Doc. 21)

   Caption title.

[Kan 6]
Lane, James H.
   . . . Answer to the President's message. [House of Representatives, Lawrence, February 13, 1858. Gen. Lane's answer to the
special message of the President of the United States, transmitting
the Lecompton Constitution to the Senate. [n. p., 1858?]
   Broadside.

   Lawrence *Republican* extra.

[Kan 7]
U. S. Congress. Senate. Committee on Territories.
   . . . Report (to accompany bill S. 161) [of] the Committee on
Territories, to whom was referred the message of the President,

[Kan 7, cont.]
communicating a constitution for Kansas as a state, adopted by
the convention which met at Lecompton, on Monday, the 4th of
September, 1857 . . . [Washington, 1858]
    88 p. ([U. S.] 35th Cong., 1st sess. Senate. Rep. Com. 82)

Caption title.
"February 18, 1858. Ordered to be printed."
Report submitted by Mr. Green.
"Minority report [submitted by Mr. Douglas] " p. [52]-76.
"Views of the minority [submitted by Mr. Collamer and
Mr. Wade] ": p. [77]-88.

[Kan 8]
U. S. Congress. House. Select Committee of Fifteen.
    The Lecompton Constitution. In the House of Representatives,
March 10, 1858. Mr. Stephens, of Georgia, from the Select Committee of Fifteen, made the following report. [Washington?
1858?]
    16 p.

Caption title.

[Kan 9]
U. S. Congress. House. Select Committee of Fifteen.
    Kansas constitution. May 11, 1858. Ordered to be printed.
Mr. A. H. Stephens, of Georgia, from the Select Committee [of
Fifteen], and the following report [containing journal and text
of the Lecompton Constitution prepared by the convention,
November 7, 1857, as well as facts connected with the formation
of Lecompton Constitution and facts bearing upon the question
of the admission of Kansas as a state under the Lecompton
Constitution. Washington? 1858?]
    319 p. ([U. S.] 35th Cong., 1st sess. House. Rept. 377)

Caption title.

[Kan 10]
Kansas (Ter.) Constitutional Convention, 1858.
. . . Constitution adopted by the convention held at Leaven-
worth. A certified copy of the constitution adopted at Leaven-
worth, in the territory of Kansas, and a schedule of the votes for
the constitution and state officers. [Washington, 1859]
    24 p., table. ([U. S.] 35th Cong., 2d sess. House. Misc. Doc. 44)

    Caption title.

[Kan 11]
Kansas (Ter.) Constitutional Convention, 1859.
    Proceedings and debates. Embracing the secretary's journal
of the Kansas constitutional convention, convened at Wyandot[te], July 5, 1859, under the act of the territorial legislature,
entitled "An act providing for the formation of a state government for the state of Kansas." Approved February 11, 1859. By
Ariel E. Drapier, reporter. Printed by order of the convention,
from the columns of the Commercial Gazette. Wyandot[te],
1859.
    2 p. l., xlvi, 439, 16 p.

    "Constitution of the state of Kansas; adopted . . . July 29,
1859": 16 p. at end.

[Kan 12]
Kansas (Ter.) Constitutional Convention, 1859.
    Kansas constitutional convention. A reprint of the proceedings
and debates of the convention which framed the constitution of
Kansas at Wyandotte in July, 1859. Also, the constitution annotated to date, historical sketches, etc. By authority of the
state legislature. Topeka, 1920.
    771 p. incl. tables.

    Compiled under the direction of State Librarians James L.
King and Winfield Freeman, by Harry G. Larimer, Bill Drafter,
and chief of Legislative Reference Library.

[Kan 12, cont.]
Binder's title: Wyandotte constitutional convention. Kansas. 1859.
"Constitution of the State of Kansas; adopted at Wyandot[te], July 29, 1859": p. 574-592.
Bibliography: p. 715-727.

[Kan 13]
U. S. Congress. House. Committee on the Territories.
. . . Kansas . . . Report . . . [Washington, 1860]
55 p. ([U. S.] 36th Cong., 1st sess. House. Rept. 255)

Caption title.
Majority report submitted by Galusha A. Grow and others; minority report by John B. Clark.
Reports and documents relating to the constitution adopted by the people of Kansas October 4, 1859, and the memorial of the convention praying Congress to admit Kansas as a state.

[Kan 14]
Kansas. Legislative Council. Research Dept.
Memorandum brief of questions that may arise in connection with the Kansas constitution and Title I of the federal Social Security Act [March 26, 1936] by Franklin Corrick . . . [n. p., 1936]
9 numb. l.

Caption title.
[Its special reports, 5]

[Kan 15]
Kansas. Commission on Constitution Revision.
Progress report . . . submitted to . . . governor of the state of Kansas and the Kansas legislature. January 30, 1959. [Topeka ? 1959]
12 p.

John M. Murray, chairman.

[Kan 16]
Kansas. Constitution.
Constitution of the state of Kansas, and amendments and proposed amendments. [Topeka] 1959.
32 p.

Kentucky

[Ky 1]
Kentucky. Constitutional Convention, 1792.
Journal of the first constitutional convention of Kentucky, held in Danville, Kentucky, April 2 to 19, 1792. Published in commemoration of Kentucky's sesquicentennial anniversary, June 1, 1942, by the State Bar Association of Kentucky. Lexington, 1942.
xii, 28 p., facsim.

Constitution: p. 11-22.

[Ky 2]
Kentucky. Constitutional Convention, 1799.
Journal of the convention. Begun and held at the Capitol in the town of Frankfort on Monday the twenty-second day of July . . . one thousand seven hundred and ninety-nine. [Frankfort, 1799?]
p. [3]-50.

No title page.

[Ky 3]
Kentucky. Constitution.
The constitution, or form of government for the state of Kentucky. Published by order of the convention. Frankfort, 1799.
48 p.

[Ky 4]
Kentucky. Constitutional Convention, 1849-1850.
Journal and proceedings of the convention of the state of Kentucky . . . Frankfort, 1849 [1850]
531 p.

"Convention called for the purpose of re-adopting, altering, or amending the Constitution of . . . Kentucky." Met October 1, 1849; adjourned June 11, 1850.

[Ky 5]
Kentucky. Constitutional Convention, 1849-1850.
Report of the debates and proceedings of the convention for the revision of the constitution of the state of Kentucky. 1849. P. Sutton, official reporter to the convention . . . Frankfort, 1849 [1850]
1168 p.

Convention met October 1, 1849; adjourned June 11, 1850. "Constitution of Kentucky": p. 1130-1142.

[Ky 6]
Kentucky. Constitution.
Text of Kentucky constitutions of 1792, 1799, and 1850 . . . Frankfort, 1965.
1 p. l., ii, 44 p. (Kentucky. Legislative Research Commission. Informational bulletin 41)

[Ky 7]
Kentucky (Provisional government, 1861-1865) Constitutional Convention.
Proceedings of the convention establishing provisional government of Kentucky. Constitution of the provisional government. Letter of the governor to the President. President's message recommending the admission of Kentucky as a member of the Confederate states. Act of Congress admitting Kentucky as a member

[Ky 7, cont.]
of the Confederate states. Acts of the provisional government
passed at Bowling Green. Codified and arranged by J. P. Burnside,
P. B. Thompson, Com. Augusta, Ga., 1863.
    39 p.

[Ky 8]
Kentucky. Constitutional Convention, 1890-1891.
    Official report of the proceedings and debates in the convention
assembled at Frankfort, on the eighth day of September, 1890, to
adopt, amend, or change the constitution of the state of Kentucky
. . . Frankfort, 1890 [1891]
    4 v. (6480 p.)

    Convention met September 8, 1890; adjourned September 28,
1891.
    "Constitution of the Commonwealth of Kentucky, adopted by
the Constitutional Convention, September 28, 1891": v. 4,
p. 6024-6052.

[Ky 9]
Kentucky. Constitution Review Commission.
    Report. [Frankfort] 1950.
    95 p.

[Ky 10]
Kentucky. Constitution.
    The constitution of Kentucky, published, with an explanatory
essay, by James T. Fleming. 6th ed. Frankfort, 1967.
    xxiv, 49 p. (Kentucky. Legislative Research Commission. Infor-
mational bulletin 59)

    Cover title: Constitution of the commonwealth of Kentucky.

Louisiana

[La 1]
Orleans (Ter.) Constitutional Convention, 1811-1812.
Journal de la Convention d'Orleans de 1811-12. Imprimé
par Jérome Bayon, pour l'usage de la Convention de 1844. Jackson, Le., 3 aout 1814. [Nouvelle-Orelans?] 1844. [Washington, 1931?]
19 p.

Cover title.

[La 2]
Orleans (Ter.) Constitutional Convention, 1811-1812.
Orleans convention . . . a memorial to Congress, praying the
annexation of Florida to this territory . . . [New Orleans, 1811?]
Broadside.

Includes "Remarks on the Florida resolution."

[La 3]
Louisiana. Constitution.
Constitution or form of government of the state of Louisiana
. . . New Orleans, 1812.
32 p.

[La 4]
Louisiana. Constitutional Convention, 1844-1845.
Journal of the convention called for the purpose of re-adopting, amending, or changing the constitution of the state of Louisiana [convened at Jackson, August 5, 1844. n. p., 1845]
72 p.

No title page.
Includes journal proceedings from August 5, 1844 to January 17, 1845.

[La 5]
Louisiana. Constitutional Convention, 1844-1845.
Journal of the proceedings of the convention of the state of Louisiana, begun and held in the city of New Orleans, on the 14th day of January, 1845. Published by authority. New Orleans, 1845.
356 p., fold. table.

The convention held meetings at Jackson, August 5-24, 1844; reassembled at New Orleans, January 14, 1845; and adjourned May 16, 1845.
Constitution of the state of Louisiana: p. 325-356.

[La 6]
Louisiana. Constitutional Convention, 1844-1845.
Official report of debates in the Louisiana convention. [August 5, 1844-January 17, 1845. New Orleans? 1845?]
146 p.

No title page; text ends abruptly in the midst of debates of January 17, 1845.

[La 7]
Louisiana. Constitutional Convention, 1844-1845.
Proceedings and debates of the convention of Louisiana, which assembled at the city of New Orleans January 14, 1844 (i.e., 1845). Robert J. Ker, reporter. New Orleans, 1845.
960 (i.e., 952), ii p.

No. 5-12 omitted paging.
The convention held meetings at Jackson, August 5-24, 1844;

[La 7, cont.]
reassembled at New Orleans, January 14, 1845; and adjourned
May 16, 1845.

This volume contains the proceedings and debates . . . from
January 14 to May 16, 1845.

"Constitution of . . . Louisiana. Adopted in convention May 14,
1845": p. 951-960.

[La 8]
Louisiana. Constitution.

The new constitution of the state of Louisiana: adopted in convention on the fourteenth of May, 1845, and ratified by the
people of the state on the fifth of November, 1845. With a comparative view of the old and new constitutions of the state a
copious index. By S. F. Glenn. New Orleans, 1845.

36, iv p.

[La 9]
Louisiana State Law Institute.

The projet of a constitution for the state of Louisiana. [Baton
Rouge] 1950.

63 p.

[La 10]
Louisiana. Constitutional Convention, 1852.

Journal of the convention to form a new constitution for the
state of Louisiana. Official. New Orleans, 1852.

100 p.

Constitution: p. 91-99.

[La 11]
Louisiana. Constitution.

Constitution of the state of Louisiana. Adopted in convention: July 31, 1852. New Orleans, 1852.

37 p.

[La 12]
Louisiana. Convention, 1861.
Official journal of the proceedings of the convention of the
state of Louisiana. By authority. New Orleans, 1861.
330 p.

"Constitution of the Confederate States of America": p. 79-85.
"Ordinances passed by the Convention . . . New Orleans, 1861"
[English and French] p. [226]-292 (i.e., 293).
"Constitution of the State of Louisiana as amended by the
State Convention of 1861. New Orleans, 1861": p. [295]-330.

[La 13]
Louisiana. Constitutional Convention, 1864.
Official journal of the proceedings of the convention for the
revision and amendment of the constitution of the state of
Louisiana. By authority. New Orleans, 1864.
184, [1], x p.

"Constitution of the State of Louisiana. Adopted in convention, July 23, 1864": p. [173]-184.

[La 14]
Louisiana. Constitutional Convention, 1864.
Debates in the convention for the revision and amendment of
the constitution of the state of Louisiana. Assembled at Liberty
Hall, New Orleans, April 6, 1864. By Albert P. Bennett, official
reporter . . . New Orleans, 1864.
643 p.

"Constitution of the state of Louisiana. Adopted in convention
July 23, 1864": p. [631]-643.

[La 15]
Louisiana. Constitutional Convention, 1867-1868.
Official journal of the proceedings of the convention, for fram-
ing a constitution for the state of Louisiana. By authority. New
Orleans, 1867-1868.
315, [1] p.
Constitution: p. 293-310.

[La 16]
Louisiana. Constitution.
Constitution adopted by the state constitutional convention of the state of Louisiana, March 7, 1868 . . . New Orleans, 1868.
22 p.

[La 17]
Louisiana. Constitutional Convention, 1879.
Official journal of the proceedings of the constitutional convention of the state of Louisiana, held in New Orleans, Monday, April 21, 1879. By authority. New Orleans, 1879.
337, 156 p., fold. tables.

[La 18]
Louisiana. Constitutional Convention, 1879.
Rules of order of the constitutional convention of the state of Louisiana, held in New Orleans, Monday, April 21, 1879 . . . New Orleans, 1879.
13, [1] p.

[La 19]
Louisiana. Constitution.
Constitution of the state of Louisiana, adopted in convention at . . . New Orleans, the twenty-third day of July, A. D. 1879. New Orleans, 1879.
90 p.

[La 20]
Louisiana. Constitution.
The constitution of the state of Louisiana, adopted in 1879, and promulgated January 1, 1880. To which are added useful and abundant annotations and references to the decisions of the Supreme Court, up to and including volume XXXIV of the annual reports, and also references to the acts of the legislature up to and including the session of 1882. Compiled and edited by Edmond Augustus Peyroux . . . New Orleans, 1883.
60 p.

Interleaved with ruled paper.

[La 21]
Louisiana. Constitutional Convention, 1898.
Official journal of the proceedings of the constitutional convention of the state of Louisiana, held in New Orleans, Tuesday, February 8, 1898. And calendar. By authority. New Orleans, 1898.
    385, iv, 77 p., fold. table.

[La 22]
Louisiana. Constitution.
Constitution of the state of Louisiana, adopted in convention at the city of New Orleans, May 12, 1898. By authority. New Orleans, 1898.
    144, xv, 29, [3] p.

    "Amendments to Constitution of 1898," 1899-1906: 29 p. at end.

[La 23]
Louisiana. Constitution.
Constitution of the state of Louisiana, adopted May 12, 1898; with amendments including the extra session of the Louisiana legislature held August 12, 1912. Annotated by Theodore Cotonio. New Orleans, 1913.
    462, xl p.

[La 24]
Louisiana. Constitutional Convention, 1913.
Official journal of the proceedings of the constitutional convention of the state of Louisiana, held at Baton Rouge, Louisiana, November 10-22, 1913 [and calendar . . .] By authority . . . Baton Rouge, 1913.
    78, 1 l., 21, [3] p.

[La 25]
Louisiana. Constitution.
Constitution of the state of Louisiana, adopted in convention at the city of Baton Rouge, November 22, 1913. By authority. Baton Rouge, 1913.
    132, xxviii p.

[La 26]
Louisiana. Constitution.
Constitution of Louisiana of 1913, with all amendments up to 1917, annotated by Robert H. Marr. Constitution of the United States as amended to May 1, 1913, annotated. New Orleans [c1917]
   348, 125 p.

The Constitution of the United States has special title page and separate paging (125 p. at end).

[La 27]
Louisiana. Constitutional Convention, 1921.
Official journal of the proceedings of the constitutional convention of the state of Louisiana. Begun and held in the city of Baton Rouge March 1, 1921. And calendar. By authority. [Baton Rouge, 1922?]
   1088, 182 p.

[La 28]
Louisiana. Constitution.
Constitution of the state of Louisiana adopted in convention at the city of Baton Rouge. June 18, 1921. By authority. [Baton Rouge, 1922?]
   xvii, 131, 32 p., facsims.

[La 29]
Louisiana. Constitution.
Constitutions of the state of Louisiana. Text of constitution adopted June 18, 1921, with text of corresponding articles in all the constitutions of the state, including all amendments. Compiled by Huey P. Long, governor of Louisiana. [Baton Rouge, c1930]
   1 v. (various pagings)

On spine: Compilation of the constitutions of the state of Louisiana (with amendments), 1812-1930.

[La 30]
Louisiana State Law Institute.
Projet of a constitution for the state of Louisiana, with notes and studies. Prepared and submitted . . . pursuant to Act 52 of 1946. August, 1954. [Baton Rouge, c1954]
4 v. in 5, map (on lining papers)

Bibliography: v. 4, p. [879]-940.

[La 31]
Louisiana. Legislative Council.
Constitutional revision in Louisiana; an analysis . . . [Baton Rouge? 1954?]
1 p. l., 39 numb. l. (Its research study no. 3)

Cover title.
At head of title: Robert A. Ainsworth, Jr., chairman; Clarence C. Aycock, vice-chairman; Emmett Asseff, executive director.

[La 32]
Louisiana. Constitution.
Constitution of the state of Louisiana, as amended through the election of November 2, 1954. Adopted in convention [June 18, 1921] at the city of Baton Rouge, Wade O. Martin, Jr., secretary of state. [Baton Rouge, 1955]
xiv, 691 p.

Maine

The debates and journal of the constitutional convention of the state of Maine, 1819-1820. And amendments subsequently made to the constitution. Augusta, 1894.
1 v. (various pagings), facsims.

Contents: ——The debates, resolutions, and other proceedings of the convention of delegates, assembled at Portland on the 11th and continued until the 29th day of October, 1819, for the purpose of forming a constitution for the state of Maine, to which is prefixed the constitution. Taken in convention by Jeremiah Perley. Portland, 1820. 436 p. ——Journal of the constitutional convention of the district of Maine, with the Articles of Separation and Governor Brooks' proclamation prefixed. 1819-1820. Augusta, 1894. 135 p. ——The Brunswick Convention of 1816. Minutes taken and preserved by William Allen, Jr., a member of the convention. p. 1-12 at end. ——Constitution of the state of Maine, formed in convention, October 29, and adopted by the people in town meetings, December 6, A. D., 1819, together with the xxi amendments subsequently made thereto, arranged as amended, in pursuance of a legislative resolve of February 24, 1875, by the chief justice of the Supreme Judicial Court, (the Honorable John Appleton) . . . and with amendments adopted since the last named date. p. [13]-56 at end. ——Biographical sketches of members of the convention, compiled expressly for this edition. p. [57]-120 at end.

[Me 2]
Maine (District) Constitutional Convention, 1819.
    Petition of a convention of the people of the district of Maine, praying to be admitted into the Union as a separate and independent state, accompanied with a constitution for said state. December 8, 1819. Read and referred to a select committee. Washington, 1819.
    35 p. ([U. S.] 16th Cong., 1st sess. House. Doc. 3)
    "Constitution of Maine": p. 7-29.

[Me 3]
Maine. Constitution.
    The constitution of the state of Maine, and that of the United States; with marginal references: containing the census of the several towns and plantations in Maine in 1820. Portland, 1831.
    94 p.

[Me 4]
Maine. Constitution.
    Proposed constitutional amendment, 1944, submitted by the 91st Legislature and to be voted upon September 11, 1944. [n. p., 1944?]
    [3] p.

[Me 5]
Maine. Secretary of State.
    Referendum questions (local option) and proposed constitutional amendments (including brief explanatory statements by the attorney general as to intent and content of each proposed constitutional amendment). . . . To be voted upon at the state election, Monday, September 13, 1954. [Augusta ?]
    12 p.

[Me 6]
Maine. Secretary of State.
    Referendum questions and proposed constitutional amendments

[Me 6, cont.]
in accordance with acts and resolves passed by the 97th Legislature, including brief explanatory statements by the attorney general as to intent and content of each proposed constitutional amendment and referendum question. . . . To be voted upon at the special election, Monday, September 12, 1955. [Augusta?] 1955.
   12 p.

[Me 7]
Maine. Constitution.
   Constitution of the state of Maine, as amended January 1, 1955 [with amendments adopted 1955 and 1957. Augusta, 1955-1957]
      30, 4, [1] p.

   Caption title.

Maryland

[Md 1]
Maryland (Colony) Convention.
Proceedings of the conventions of the province of Maryland, held at the city of Annapolis, in 1774, 1775, and 1776. Baltimore, Annapolis, 1836.
378 p.

In accordance with a resolution of the June 21-July 6, 1776 convention calling for a constitutional convention, a constitution was framed by the convention of August 14, 1776.
Declaration of rights: p. 311-316; constitution: p. 349-363.

[Md 2]
Maryland. Constitution.
The constitution and form of government, as proposed to be amended by a committee appointed by the House of Delegates at the last session. Annapolis [1792]
25 p.

[Md 3]
Maryland. Constitution.
Amendments to the constitution of 1776 [ratified 1792, 1795, 1798, 1799, 1803, 1805, 1807, 1809, 1810, 1812, 1837, and 1846]

[Md 3, cont.]

(In Thorpe, Francis Newton, comp. The federal and state constitutions, colonial charters, and other organic laws of the states, territories, and colonies now or heretofore forming the United States of America. Washington, 1909. v. 3, p. 1701-1712)

[Md 4]
Maryland. Constitutional Convention, 1850-1851.
Proceedings of the Maryland state convention, to frame a new constitution. Commenced at Annapolis, November 4, 1850. Annapolis, 1850 [1851]
895, 8 p.

With this is bound [Md 9] "The Constitution of the State of Maryland reported and adopted by the Convention of Delegates ... 1850 ... Annapolis, 1851." 36 p.

[Md 5]
Maryland. Constitutional Convention, 1850-1851.
Debates and proceedings of the Maryland reform convention to revise the state constitution. To which are prefixed the Bill of Rights and the constitution as adopted. Annapolis, 1851.
2 v.

[Md 6]
Maryland. Constitutional Convention, 1850-1851.
Rules and orders for the regulation and government of the state convention of Maryland. Annapolis, 1850.
7 p.

[Md 7]
Maryland. Constitutional Convention, 1850-1851.
Report of the Committee on the Fugitive Slave Case. [Annapolis? 1851]
20 p.

Includes the correspondence of the governor of Pennsylvania and the governor of Maryland on the delivery of James S. Mitchell on indictment of kidnapping.

[Md 8]
Maryland. Constitutional Convention, 1850-1851.
Speeches delivered at a dinner given to the Hon. Daniel Webster
by the reform convention of Maryland, at Annapolis, Tuesday,
March 25, 1851. Washington, 1851.
21 p.

[Md 9]
Maryland. Constitution.
The constitution of the state of Maryland, reported and adopted
by the convention of delegates assembled at the city of Annapolis,
November 4, 1850, and submitted to the voters of the state for
their adoption or rejection, on the first Wednesday of June, 1851.
Annapolis, 1851.
36 p. [With (Md 4) Maryland. Constitutional convention, 1850-
1851. Proceedings. Annapolis, 1850 (1951)]

[Md 10]
Maryland. Constitution.
The constitution of the state of Maryland, reported and adopted
by the convention of delegates assembled at the city of Annapolis,
November 4, 1850, and submitted to and ratified by the people on
the first Wednesday of June, 1851, with marginal notes and ref-
erences . . . and an appendix and index. By Edward Otis Hinkley
. . . Baltimore, 1855.
108 p.
"Appendix to second edition": p. [75]-82.

[Md 11]
Maryland. Constitutional Convention, 1864.
Proceedings of the state convention of Maryland to frame a new
constitution. Commenced at Annapolis, April 27, 1864. Annapolis, 1864.
856 p.

[Md 12]
Maryland. Constitutional Convention, 1864.
    The debates of the constitutional convention of the state of Maryland, assembled at the city of Annapolis, Wednesday, April 27, 1864: being a full and complete report of the debates and proceedings of the convention, together with the old constitution, the law under which the convention assembled and the new constitution. Official: Wm. Blair Lord, reporter—Harry M. Parkhurst, assistant . . . Annapolis, 1864.
    3 v. (1988 p.)

[Md 13]
Maryland. Constitution.
    The constitution of the state of Maryland. Reported and adopted by the convention of delegates assembled at the city of Annapolis, April 27, 1864, and submitted to and ratified by the people on the 12th and 13th days of October, 1864. With marginal notes and references to acts of the General Assembly and decisions of the Court of Appeals, and an appendix and index, by Edward Otis Hinkley . . . Baltimore, 1865.
    102, [1] p.

[Md 14]
Maryland. Constitutional Convention, 1867.
    Proceedings of the state convention of Maryland, to frame a new constitution, commenced at Annapolis, May 8, 1867. Annapolis, May 8, 1867. Annapolis, 1867.
    850, [96] p.

[Md 15]
Maryland. Constitutional Convention, 1867.
    Debates of the Maryland constitutional convention of 1867 (as reprinted from articles reported in the Baltimore Sun.) Compiled by Philip B. Perlman . . . Baltimore [c1923]
    636 p.

    "The Sun's reports of convention written by Frank A. Richardson."

[Md 16]
Maryland. Constitutional Convention, 1867.
Rules and orders for the regulation and government of the constitutional convention of 1867. Annapolis, 1867.
12 p.

[Md 17]
Maryland. Constitution.
The constitution of the state of Maryland. Formed and adopted by the convention which assembled at the city of Annapolis, May 8, 1867, and submitted to and ratified by the people on the 18th day of September, 1867. With marginal notes and references, to acts of the General Assembly and decisions of the Court of Appeals, and an appendix and index. By Edward Otis Hinkley . . . Baltimore, 1867.
156 p.

[Md 18]
Maryland. Commission on the Judiciary Article of the Constitution of Maryland.
Interim report of the Commission on the Judiciary Article of the Constitution of Maryland. [Baltimore] 1942.
14 p.

Cover title.

[Md 19]
Maryland. Commission on the Judiciary Article of the Constitution of Maryland.
Report of the Commission on the Judiciary Article of the Constitution of Maryland. [Baltimore] 1942.
16 p.

Cover title.
Report of the commission's conclusions and recommendations. Cf. p. [1]

[Md 20]
Maryland. Constitution.
Constitution of Maryland.

(In Maryland. Secretary of state. Maryland manual, 1959-1960.
[Baltimore, c1960] p. 425-537)

Massachusetts

[Ma 1]
Massachusetts (Colony) Committee of Convention.
   A report of a Committee of Convention of a form of government for the state of Massachusetts-Bay, published for the inspection and perusal of the members. [Boston? 1777]
   8 p.

[Ma 2]
Massachusetts (Colony) General Court.
   Result of the convention of delegates holden at Ipswich in the county of Essex, who were deputed to take into consideration the constitution and form of government, proposed by the convention of the state of Massachusetts-Bay. Newbury-port, 1778.
   68 p.

   In accordance with a recommendation of the General Court of the previous year, the General Court of 1777-1778 met together as a convention and adopted a constitution.

[Ma 3]
Massachusetts (Colony) General Court.
   A constitution and form of government for the state of Massachusetts-Bay. Agreed upon by the convention of said state, February 28, 1778, to be laid before the several towns and plantations

[Ma 3, cont.]

in said state, for their approbation or disapprobation. Boston, 1778.

23 p.

Rejected on submission to the people.

[Ma 4]

Massachusetts. Constitutional Convention, 1779-1780.

Journal of the convention for framing a constitution of government for the state of Massachusetts-Bay, from the commencement of the first session, September 1, 1779, to the close of their last session, June 16, 1780, including a list of the members. Boston, 1832.

264 p.

With an appendix containing: The resolve for ascertaining the sense of the people on the subject of a new constitution; the form of government originally reported by the general committee of the convention; the address to the people; the constitution as finally agreed upon by the convention, and ratified by the people, with the amendments since adopted; the rejected constitution of 1778.

[Ma 5]

Massachusetts. Constitutional Convention, 1779-1780.

The report of a constitution, or form of government for the commonwealth of Massachusetts: agreed upon by the committee, to be laid before the convention of delegates, assembled at Cambridge, on the first day of September, A. D. 1779, and continued by adjournment to the twenty-eighth day of October following. Boston, 1779.

50 p.

Cover title: The report of the Committee of Convention.

[Ma 6]

Massachusetts. Constitutional Convention, 1779-1780.

An address of the convention, for framing a new constitution of government, for the state of Massachusetts-Bay, to their constituents. Boston, 1780.

18 p.

[Ma 7]
Massachusetts. Constitution.
    A constitution or frame of government, agreed upon by the delegates of the people of the state of Massachusetts-Bay, in convention begun and held at Cambridge on the first of September, 1779, and continued by adjournments to the second of March, 1780. To be submitted to the revision of their constituents, in order to the compleating of the same, in conformity to their amendments, at a session to be held for that purpose, on the first Wednesday in June next ensuing. Boston, 1780.
    53 p.

[Ma 8]
Massachusetts. Constitutional Convention, 1779-1780.
    State of Massachusetts-Bay. In convention, June 16, 1780. Whereas, upon due examination of the returns made by the several towns and plantations . . . This convention do hereupon declare the said form to be the constitution of government . . .
[Boston, 1780]
    Broadside.

[Ma 9]
Massachusetts. Constitution.
    The constitution of the state of Massachusetts, adopted 1780. [With an act relating to the calling a convention of delegates of the people, for the purpose of revising the constitution. Approved by the governor, June 16, 1820] Boston; 1820.
    60 p.

[Ma 10]
Massachusetts. General Court.
    [Report of] the committee of both Houses, to whom was referred so much of the message of His Excellency the Governor, as relates to such amendment of the constitution of this commonwealth, or such modification of the laws thereof, as may be necessary to meet the exigency resulting from the secession of Maine.
[Boston? 1820]
    8 p.

[Ma 11]
Massachusetts. Constitutional Convention, 1820-1821.
Journal of debates and proceedings in the convention of delegates, chosen to revise the constitution of Massachusetts, begun and holden at Boston, November 15, 1820, and continued by adjournment to January 9, 1821. Reported for the Boston Daily Advertiser. New ed., rev. and cor. Boston, 1853.
vii, 677 p.

Edited by Nathan and Charles Hale.

[Ma 12]
Massachusetts. Constitutional Convention, 1820-1821.
Rules and orders to be observed in the convention of delegates, for the commonwealth of Massachusetts, which met on Wednesday, November 15, 1820. Boston, 1820.
36 p.

[Ma 13]
Massachusetts. Constitutional Convention, 1820-1821.
Amendments of the constitution of Massachusetts, proposed by the convention of delegates, assembled at Boston, on the third Wednesday of November, A. D. eighteen hundred and twenty. With their address to the people of this commonwealth. Boston, 1821.
32 p.

[Ma 14]
Massachusetts. Constitution.
Constitution or form of government for the commonwealth of Massachusetts—1780 [as amended in 1820, 1822, 1833, 1836, and 1840]

(In Thorpe, Francis Newton, comp. The federal and state constitutions, colonial charters, and other organic laws of the states, territories, and colonies now or heretofore forming the United States of America. Washington, 1909. v. 3, p. 1888-1922)

[Ma 15]
Massachusetts. Constitutional Convention, 1853.
Journal of the constitutional convention of the commonwealth of Massachusetts, begun and held in Boston, on the fourth day of May, 1853. Boston, 1853.
560 p.

[Ma 16]
Massachusetts. Constitutional Convention, 1853.
Official report of the debates and proceedings in the state convention, assembled May 4, 1853, to revise and amend the constitution of the commonwealth of Massachusetts. Boston, 1853.
3 v.

[Ma 17]
Massachusetts. Constitutional Convention, 1853.
Discussions on the constitution proposed to the people of Massachusetts by the convention of 1853. Boston, 1854.
306 p.

Contents.—Letters of Phocion, by G. T. Curtis.—Letters of Silas Standfast, by G. S. Hillard.—Address of Samuel Hoar, at Fitchberg.—Address of Marcus Morton, at Taunton.—Address of C. F. Adams, at Quincy.—Remarks, by J. G. Palfrey.

[Ma 18]
Massachusetts. Constitutional Convention, 1853.
Documents printed by order of the constitutional convention of the commonwealth of Massachusetts, during the session, A. D. 1853. Boston, 1853.
1 v. (various pagings)

[Ma 19]
Massachusetts. Constitutional Convention, 1853.
Rules and orders to be observed in the convention of delegates for the commonwealth of Massachusetts, met on Wednesday, the 4th day of May, 1853. Boston, 1853.
136, [1] p. diagr.

[Ma 20]
Massachusetts. Constitution.
Constitution of the commonwealth of Massachusetts. Published in conformity to a resolve of the legislature of April 26, 1853. Boston, 1853.
46 p.

The constitution was rejected.

[Ma 21]
Massachusetts. Constitution.
Amendments to the constitution of 1780 [ratified 1855, 1857, 1859, 1860, and 1863]

(In Poore, Ben. Perley, comp. The federal and state constitutions, colonial charters, and other organic laws of the United States. Washington, 1877. v. 1, p. 977-980)

[Ma 22]
Massachusetts. Constitution.
Constitution or form of government for the commonwealth of Massachusetts, 1916.

(In Massachusetts. General Court. Manual for the use of the General Court. Boston, 1916. p. 25-90)

[Ma 23]
Massachusetts. Constitutional Convention, 1917-1919.
Journal of the constitutional convention of the commonwealth of Massachusetts. 1917 . . . Boston, 1917-[19—?]
970 p.

[Ma 24]
Massachusetts. Constitutional Convention, 1917-1919.
Debates in the Massachusetts constitutional convention, 1917-1919. Boston, 1918-1920.

[Ma 25]
Massachusetts. Constitutional Convention, 1917-1919.
[Bulletins, no. 1-26. Elliot H. Paul, editor. Boston, 1917-1919]
1 v. (various pagings)

[Ma 26]
Massachusetts. Commission to Compile Information and Data for the Use of the Constitutional Convention.
[Bulletins] submitted to the constitutional convention by the Commission to Compile Information and Data for the Use of the Constitutional Convention. Boston, 1917.
3 v.

[Ma 27]
Massachusetts. Commission to Compile Information and Data for the Use of the Constitutional Convention.
A manual for the constitutional convention, 1917, submitted to the constitutional convention by the Commission to Compile Information and Data for the Use of the Constitutional Convention. 2d ed. Boston, 1917.
302 p., folded facsim.

[Ma 28]
Massachusetts. Governor, 1916-1919 (Samuel W. McCall)
A proclamation promulgating the articles of amendment to the constitution submitted to the people by the constitutional convention, November 5, 1918. [Boston? 1918?]
xv p.

[Ma 29]
Massachusetts. Constitutional Convention, 1917-1919.
Amendments passed by the constitutional convention for submission to the people at the election to be held November 5, 1918. Together with an explanatory address by the president of the convention, John L. Bates. Boston, 1918.
20 p.

[Ma 30]
Massachusetts. Secretary of the Commonwealth.

Text of the rearrangement of the constitution submitted by the constitutional convention, together with referendum questions submitted to voters under amendments to the constitution, article XLVIII, general provisions, IV, information to voters. State election, November 4, 1919. Boston, 1919.

32 p.

[Ma 31]
Massachusetts. Constitution.

Constitution or form of government for the commonwealth of Massachusetts [1959]

(In Massachusetts. General Court. Manual for the use of the General Court for 1959-1960. Boston, 1959. p. [37]-143)

Michigan

[Mi 1]
Michigan. Constitutional Convention, 1835.
Journal of the proceedings of the convention to form a constitution for the state of Michigan; begun and held at the Capitol, in the city of Detroit, on Monday, the 11th day of May, A. D. 1835. Printed by order of the convention. Detroit, 1835.
224, vii p.

[Mi 2]
Michigan. Constitutional Convention, 1835.
The Michigan constitutional conventions of 1835-1836; debates and proceedings, edited by Harold M. Dorr . . . Ann Arbor, London, 1940.
xi, 626 p., 2 tables (1 fold.). University of Michigan publications. History and political science, v. XIII)

"Bibliographical note": p. 610-611.

[Mi 3]
Michigan. Constitutional Convention, 1835.
Appeal by the convention of Michigan, to the people of the United States; with other documents, in relation to the boundary question between Michigan and Ohio. Printed for the convention. Detroit, 1835.
176 p.

[Mi 4]
Michigan. Constitution.
Constitution of the state of Michigan as adopted in convention, begun and held at the Capitol, in the city of Detroit, on Monday, the 11th day of May, A. D. 1835 . . . Detroit, 1835.
20 p.

Printed by order of the convention.

[Mi 5]
Michigan. Constitutional Convention, 1850.
Journal of the constitutional convention of the state of Michigan. 1850. Printed by order of the convention, under the supervision of John Swegles, Jr., principal secretary of the convention, Lansing, 1850.
581, [77] p.

The appendix contains documents of the convention, no. 1-8 (various pagings).
"Constitution of the State of Michigan": p. 524-560.

[Mi 6]
Michigan. Constitutional Convention, 1850.
Report of the proceedings and debates in the convention to revise the constitution of the state of Michigan. 1850. Lansing, 1850.
xliii p., 2 l., 937, [1] p.

"Revised constitution, 1850": p. [xxiii]-xliii.

[Mi 7]
Michigan. Constitutional Convention, 1867.
Journal of the constitutional convention of the state of Michigan, 1867. Printed by order of the convention, under the supervision of Thomas H. Glenn, principal secretary of the convention. By authority. Lansing, 1867.
943 p.

Revised constitution: p. 841-874. This constitution was rejected by the people.

[Mi 8]
Michigan. Constitutional Convention, 1867.
The debates and proceedings of the constitutional convention of the state of Michigan, convened at the city of Lansing, Wednesday, May 15, 1867. Official report by Wm. Blair Lord and David Wolfe Brown. Lansing, 1867.

"The new constitution": v. 2, p. 1008-1017. This constitution was rejected by the people.

[Mi 9]
Michigan. Constitutional Convention, 1867.
Manual of the constitutional convention of the state of Michigan. Begun in the Capitol, at Lansing, May 15, A. D. 1867.
74 p.

Published "By áuthority."
Autographs of members of the convention, on blank leaves bound in at end.

[Mi 10]
Michigan. Constitutional Commission, 1873.
Journal of the Constitutional Commission of Michigan. Printed by order of the commission, under the direction and supervision of Henry S. Clubb, clerk of the Constitutional Commission. By authority. Lansing, 1873.
243, vii, 56 p.

"Appendix: containing the report to the Governor, an index to the changes proposed, the constitution as proposed to be amended, the present Constitution."

[Mi 11]
Michigan. Constitution.
The constitution of Michigan as proposed for amendment and submitted to the people in the form of a joint resolution, with notations of proposed changes. By authority. Lansing, 1874.
50 p.

[Mi 11, cont.]

At head of title: To be voted upon Tuesday, November 3, 1874.
"The joint resolution proposing the extension of the elective franchise to women is appended as a separate proposition, and does
not depend in any manner upon the other proposed amendments.

"A brief review of the amended constitution": p. [5]-11.

[Mi 12]

Michigan. Constitution.

Constitution of the state of Michigan. 1850. Annotated for the
use of the constitutional convention of 1907. Lansing, 1907.

78 p. (Michigan. State Library. Legislative Reference Dept.
Bulletin no. 1, September, 1907)

[Mi 13]

Michigan. Constitutional Convention, 1907-1908.

Journal of the constitutional convention of the state of Michigan 1907-1908 . . . published in accordance with provisions of act
no. 272 of the public acts of 1907. Paul H. King, secretary of the
constitutional convention . . . Lansing, 1908.

2 v. (xlix, 1, 1826 p.)

[Mi 14]

Michigan. Constitutional Convention, 1907-1908.

Proceedings and debates of the constitutional convention of the
state of Michigan, convened in the city of Lansing, Tuesday, October 22, 1907 . . . Official report, by Joseph H. Brewer, Chas. H.
Bender, Chas. H. McGurrin, official stenographers of the convention. Lansing, 1907-[1908]

2 v. (1525 p.)

Adjourned March 3, 1908.

[Mi 15]

Michigan. Constitutional Convention, 1907-1908.

Handbook. Michigan constitutional convention. 1907. Compiled by Alex. H. Smith, assistant secretary, under the direction
of Paul H. King, secretary. [Lansing? 1907?]

180 p. incl. fold. diagr.

[Mi 16]
Michigan. Constitutional Convention, 1907-1908.
Manual of the constitutional convention of Michigan. Lansing
[1909?]
149 p., 29 ports.

"Biographies of the members of the Constitutional Convention
of 1907": p. [89]-142.
Constitution of 1907-1908: p. 37-86.
Eliminated sections of the constitution of 1850: p. 87-88.

[Mi 17]
Michigan. Constitutional Convention, 1907-1908.
Report of the Committee on Submission and Address to the
People, submitting the proposed revision of the present constitu-
tion of Michigan. [Lansing? 1908]
72 p.

Signed by Victor M. Gore and fourteen others (Committee on
Submission and Address to the People). Adopted by the constitutional convention, February 21, 1908.

[Mi 18]
Michigan. Constitution.
The annotated constitution of Michigan, with introduction by
Fred. A. Baker; annotations by Franklin A. Beecher. Detroit,
1909.
xxi, 158 p.

Report of Special Committee on State Constitutions: p. [9]-30.

[Mi 19]
Michigan. Constitutional Revision Study Commission.
Report of the Michigan Constitutional Revision Study Com-
mission. Hon. Murray D. Van Wagoner, governor; Hon. George
E. Bushnell, general chairman. [Lansing?] 1942.
1 v. (various pagings)

Cover title.

[Mi 20]
Michigan. Constitution.
Constitution of the state of Michigan. Compiled and published under the supervision of the secretary of state. [Lansing?] 1960.
64 p.

Minnesota

[Mn 1]
Minnesota (Ter.) Constitutional Convention, 1857.
Journal of the constitutional convention of the territory of Minnesota, begun and held in the city of Saint Paul, capital of said territory, on Monday, the thirteenth day of July, one thousand eight hundred and fifty-seven. Saint Paul, 1857.
209 p.

"Constitution of the State of Minnesota": p. [171]-196.

[Mn 2]
Minnesota (Ter.) Constitutional Convention, 1857.
The debates and proceedings of the Minnesota constitutional convention, including the organic act of Congress, the act of the territorial legislature relative to the convention, and the vote of the people on the constitution. Reported officially by Francis H. Smith. Saint Paul, 1857.
xix, 1 l., 685 p.

The Democratic and Republican sections of the convention met separately. The constitution finally adopted was the work of a joint committee. This volume contains the debates, etc., of the Democratic section.

[Mn 3]
Minnesota (Ter.) Constitutional Convention, 1857.
Debates and proceedings of the constitutional convention for the territory of Minnesota, to form a state constitution preparatory to its admission into the Union as a state. T. F. Andrews, official reporter to the convention. Saint Paul, 1858.
    7, xviii, [9]-624 p.

The Democratic and the Republican sections of the convention met separately. The constitution finally adopted was the work of a joint committee. This volume contains the debates, etc., of the Republican section.
    "Constitution of the State of Minnesota": p. 605-619.

[Mn 4]
Minnesota. Constitution.
Constitution of the state of Minnesota, with judicial constructions and interpretations by state and federal courts.

(In Minnesota. Laws, statutes, etc. Minnesota statutes annotated. St. Paul [1946-1948] v. 1-2)

[Mn 5]
Minnesota. Constitutional Commission.
Report. St. Paul, 1948.
120 p.

[Mn 6]
Minnesota. Constitution.
Constitution of the state of Minnesota. Prepared by Joseph L. Donovan, secretary of state. [St. Paul] 1957.

Mississippi

[Ms 1]
Mississippi. Constitutional Convention, 1817.
Journal of the convention of the western part of the Mississippi Territory, begun and held at the town of Washington, on the seventh day of July, 1817. Port-Gibson, 1831.
108 p.

[Ms 2]
Mississippi. Constitutional Convention, 1817.
Memorial of the Mississippi convention, praying an extension of the limits of that state. December 17, 1817 . . . Washington, 1817.
8 p. ([U. S.] 15th Cong., 1st sess. House. Doc. 15)

[Ms 3]
Mississippi. Constitution.
Constitution and form of government for the state of Mississippi.

(In Mississippi. Laws, statutes, etc. The revised code of the laws of Mississippi . . . 1824. p. 539-558)

[Ms 4]
Mississippi. Constitutional Convention, 1832.
Journal of the convention of the state of Mississippi, held in the town of Jackson. Published by authority. Jackson, 1832.
304 p.

[Ms 5]
Mississippi. Constitution.
The constitution of the state of Mississippi. As revised in convention, on the twenty-sixth day of October, A. D. 1832. Jackson, 1832.
27 p.

[Ms 6]
Mississippi. Convention, 1861.
Journal of the state convention and ordinances and resolutions adopted in January, 1861, with an appendix. Published by order of the convention. Jackson, 1861.
256 p., fold. table.

"Constitution of the State of Mississippi": p. [91]-117.
A leaf is inserted after page 50, with caption "Nota bene."
First paragraph, "In explanation of the following ballots, the printer takes the liberty of inserting the following extracts from the revised reports of the Convention, as published in the Mississippian."

[Ms 7]
Mississippi. Convention, 1861.
Journal of the state convention, and ordinances and resolutions adopted in March, 1861. Published by order of the convention. Jackson, 1861.
104 p.

"Constitution of the Confederate States:" p. [5]-20. "Constitution of the State of Mississippi": p. [49]-75.

[Ms 8]
Mississippi. Convention, 1861.
Proceedings of the Mississippi state convention, held January 7 to 26, A. D. 1861. Including the ordinances as finally adopted, important speeches, and a list of members, showing the post office, profession, nativity, politics, age, religious preference, and

[Ms 8, cont.]
social relations of each, by J. L. Power, convention reporter.
Jackson, 1861.
    128 p., port. fold.

[Ms 9]
Mississippi. Constitutional Convention, 1865.
    Journal of the proceedings and debates in the constitutional
convention of the state of Mississippi, August, 1865. By order of
the convention. Jackson, 1865.
    296, [2] p.

[Ms 10]
Mississippi. Constitution.
    Constitution of the state of Mississippi, as amended, with the
ordinances and resolutions adopted by the constitutional convention, August, 1865. By order of the convention. Jackson, 1865.
    56 p.

[Ms 11]
Mississippi. Constitutional Convention, 1868.
    Journal of the proceedings in the constitutional convention
of the state of Mississippi. 1868. Printed by order of the convention. Jackson, 1871.
    776 p.

    "The Constitution of the State of Mississippi, as adopted in con-
vention, May 15, 1868": p. 720-744.

[Ms 12]
Mississippi. Constitutional Convention, 1868.
    [Documents. Jackson? 1868]
    1 v. (various pagings)

    Contents:—No. 19. Minority report on Committee on Judiciary.
15 p.—No. 21. Minority report on Legislative Department. 3 p.—
No. 31. Report of Committee on Judiciary. 8 p.—No. 40. Report
of Committee on Legislative Department. 4 p.—No. 46. Report of
Committee on County Boundaries. 5 p.

[Ms 13]
Mississippi. Constitutional Convention, 1890.
Journal of the proceedings of the constitutional convention, of the state of Mississippi, begun at the city of Jackson on August 12, 1890, and concluded November 1, 1890. Printed by authority. Jackson, 1890.
757 p.

"Constitution of the State of Mississippi" [as adopted in convention] : p. 638-685.

[Ms 14]
Mississippi. Constitutional Convention, 1890.
Report of the committee appointed by the State Farmers' Alliance, in session at Starkville, to memorialize the constitutional convention concerning certain matters. [n. p., 1890]
1 l.

S. D. Lee, chairman for the committee.

[Ms 15]
Mississippi. Constitutional Convention, 1890.
Suffrage amendments to constitution. By Mr. Regan, of Clairborne. [Referred to Committee on Franchise n. p., 1890]
1 l.

[Ms 16]
Reunion of the Survivors of the Constitutional Convention of
    1890, Jackson, Miss., 1910.
Proceedings of a reunion of the survivors of the constitutional convention of 1890. On the thirty-seventh anniversay of the adoption of the constitution. Held in the Senate chamber of the new Capitol at Jackson, Mississippi, November 1, 1927. With notes and comments by Edgar S. Wilson, secretary. [Jackson, 1928]
63 p., ports.

"Published by the Department of Archives and History."

[Ms 17]
Mississippi. Constitution.
The constitution of the state of Mississippi, adopted by the people of Mississippi in a constitutional convention, November 1, 1890, at Jackson, and all amendments subsequently adopted, with source, reference, attorney general's opinions, and judicial decisions; compiled by J. P. Coleman, attorney general. [Jackson, cover 1954]
240 p.

Missouri

[Mo 1]
Missouri. Constitutional Convention, 1820.
  Journal of the Missouri state convention. St. Louis, 1820.
  48 p.

  Proceedings of June 12-July 19, 1820.

[Mo 2]
Missouri. Constitution.
  Constitution of the state of Missouri. November 16, 1820. Read
and referred to a select committee. Washington, 1820.
  25 p.

[Mo 3]
Missouri. Constitution.
  . . . Resolutions of the legislature of Missouri, for amending
the constitution of that state, so far as relates to the boundary
lines thereof. [Washington, 1835]
  1 l. ([U. S.] 23d Cong., 2d sess. Doc. 137)

  February 24, 1835, ordered to be printed.

[Mo 4]
Missouri. Constitutional Convention, 1845-1846.
  Journal of the convention of the state of Missouri, assembled
at . . . Jefferson on Monday the seventeenth day of November,

[Mo 4, cont.]

in the year . . . one thousand eight hundred and forty-five, pursuant to an act of the General Assembly of . . . Missouri . . . approved February 27, 1843. Printed by order of the convention. Jefferson, 1845.

366, 75 p.

"Engrossed articles, &c" [constitution] : p. 38-61.

The constitution proposed by the convention was rejected by the people.

[Mo 5]

Missouri. Constitutional Convention, 1845-1846.

Boundary line between Iowa and Missouri. Memorial of the convention of the state of Missouri on the admission of Iowa into the Union and on the northern boundary of the state of Missouri. February 5, 1846. Referred to the Committee on the Territories. [n. p., n. d.]

7 p. ([U. S.] 29th Cong., 1st sess. House. Doc. 104)

Caption title.

[Mo 6]

Missouri. Convention, March, 1861.

Journal and proceedings of the Missouri state convention held at Jefferson City and St. Louis, March, 1861. St. Louis, 1861.

65, 269 p.

[Mo 7]

Missouri. Convention, July, 1861.

Journal of the Missouri state convention held at Jefferson City, July, 1861. St. Louis, 1861.

36 p.

[Mo 8]

Missouri. Convention, July 1861.

Proceedings of the Missouri state convention held at Jefferson City, July, 1861. St. Louis, 1861.

136 p.

[Mo 9]
Missouri. Convention, October, 1861.
Journal of the Missouri state convention held at the city of St. Louis, October, 1861. St. Louis, 1861.
27 p., 1 l.

[Mo 10]
Missouri. Convention, October, 1861.
Proceedings of the Missouri state convention held at the city of St. Louis, October, 1861. St. Louis, 1861.
111 p.

[Mo 11]
Missouri. Convention, 1862.
Journal of the Missouri state convention held in Jefferson City, June, 1862. St. Louis, 1862.
51, [1], 32, 253 p.

Included are "Ordinances," printed as an appendix to the journal, and "Proceedings" with special title.

[Mo 12]
Missouri. Convention, 1863.
Journal of the Missouri state convention held in Jefferson City, June, 1863. St. Louis, 1863.
54, 16 p., 1 l.

Includes "Proceedings," 380 p.

[Mo 13]
Missouri. Constitutional Convention, 1865.
Journal of the Missouri state convention, held at the city of St. Louis, January 6-April 10, 1865. St. Louis, 1865.
287 p.

"Constitution of . . . Missouri, as revised, amended and adopted in convention . . . at . . . St. Louis . . . eighteen hundred and sixty-five": p. 255-277.

[Mo 14]
Missouri. Constitutional Convention, 1865.
List of state officers and names of the delegates to the constitutional convention of Missouri, convened in the Mercantile library building, St. Louis, Missouri, January 6, 1865 . . . St. Louis, 1865.
11, [1] p., fold. table.

At head of title: To Hon. Arnold Krekel, president of the Missouri state constitutional convention, this pamphlet of official reference to said body.
Compiled by Henry J. Stierlin, doorkeeper.

[Mo 15]
Switzler, William P.
Disfranchisement of rebels; speech of William F. Switzler of Boone County, delivered in the Missouri constitutional convention, on Friday, January 27, 1865. St. Louis, 1865.
12 p.

[Mo 16]
Missouri. Constitutional Convention, 1865.
Shall the new constitution be adopted? Explanation of votes for and against it on the final passage in the state convention, April 8, 1865. [St. Louis? 1865]

Caption title.
"Address of the minority of the Convention. To the loyal voters of Missouri": p. 6-8.

[Mo 17]
To the members of the Radical party of Missouri . . . call for a mass meeting of all radical opponents to the new constitution . . . [St. Louis, 1863, i.e., 1865]
6 p.

Caption title.

[Mo 18]
Missouri. Constitutional Convention, 1875.
Journal [of the] Missouri constitutional convention of 1875 . . .
with an historical introduction on constitutions and constitutional conventions in Missouri by Isidor Loeb . . . and a biographical account of the personnel of the convention by Floyd C.
Shoemaker, . . . editors . . . [Jefferson City, 1920]
2 v. (954 p.), fold. front., ports., tables.

A Missouri centennial publication of the State Historical Society
of Missouri.
"Biographical sketches of the delegates by Buel Leopard": v. 1,
p. 72-112.
"List of members of the Constitutional Convention, with resi-
dences, districts represented, and committees": v. 2, p. 891-909.

[Mo 19]
Missouri. Constitutional Convention, 1875.
Debates of the Missouri constitutional convention of 1875,
edited by Isidor Loeb . . . and Floyd C. Shoemaker . . . Columbia,
1930-1944.
12 v.

[Mo 20]
Missouri. Constitution.
New constitution of the state of Missouri, adopted in convention August 2, 1875; and an ordinance prohibiting the payment
of missing railroad bonds; also the address of the convention to
the people of the state. Election: Saturday, October 30, 1875.
Jefferson City, 1875.
54 p.

[Mo 21]
Missouri. Constitution.
Constitution of the state of Missouri adopted by vote of the
people, October 30, 1875. Went into operation November 30,

[Mo 21, cont.]
1875. Includes all amendments adopted by vote of the people up
to 1921. [Jefferson City, 1921]
   141 p.
   Cover title.

[Mo 22]
Missouri. Constitutional Convention, 1922-1923.
   The record of the proceedings of the Missouri constitutional
convention, year 1922, on the proposed amendment providing for
old age pensions. Issued by Joseph B. Shannon, a member thereof.
October 15, 1924. [Kansas City, 1924]
   55 p.
   Addenda slip inserted.

[Mo 23]
Missouri. Constitutional Convention, 1922-1923.
   File no. 1-[16 . . . n. p., 1922?]
   16 nos. in 1 v.

   Caption title.
   With this is bound: Its amendments to the constitution of
Missouri . . . 1923.

[Mo 24]
Missouri. Constitutional Convention, 1922-1923.
   Amendments to the constitution of Missouri, proposed by the
constitutional convention, 1922-1923, and the address to the people, to be submitted at special election to be held Tuesday, February 26, 1924. Jefferson City [1923]
   79 p. (With its File no. 1-[16 . . . 1922?])

[Mo 25]
Association for Constitutional Amendments, St. Louis, Missouri.
   ABC of the 21 constitutional amendments submitted by the
Missouri constitutional convention. Special election, February

[Mo 25, cont.]
26, 1924. A simple explanation of the proposed changes, together with form of ballot to be submitted, names of delegates to the convention. St. Louis [1924]
  [16] p.

[Mo 26]
Missouri. Constitution.
  Constitution of the state of Missouri, adopted by vote of the people October 30, 1875. Includes all amendments adopted by vote of the people up to 1935. Dwight H. Brown, secretary of state. [Jefferson City, 1935]
  136 p.

[Mo 27]
Missouri. Constitutional Convention, 1943-1944.
  Journal of the constitutional convention of Missouri, 1943-[1944] . . . September 21, 1943-[September 29, 1944. Jefferson City, 1943-1944]
  215 nos. in 3 v.

——. Indexes: 1943-1944.
  78 p.

[Mo 28]
State-wide Committee for the Revision of the Missouri Constitution.
  [Series of research reports] Columbia, 1943.
  8 v. in 1.

  Manuals for the delegates to the constitutional convention.

[Mo 29]
Missouri. Constitutional Convention, 1943-1944.
  Constitutional convention news. [For release Wednesday, December 1, 1943-September 18, 1944. Jefferson City, 1943-1944]
  28 numb. l.

  Caption title.
  Immediate Release at end.

[Mo 30]
Missouri. Constitutional Convention, 1943-1944.
    Reports of Committee no. 23 on phraseology, arrangement, and schedule of the constitution of the state of Missouri, 1945, to the Hon. Robert E. Blake, president of the 1943-1944 constitutional convention of Missouri. Jefferson City [1944]
    146 p.

    Cover title.

[Mo 31]
Missouri. Constitutional Convention, 1943-1944.
    [Explanation and comments by the Committee on Information, Submission and Address to the People. Jefferson City, 1944]
    1 v. (various pagings)

    Contents:—The new article on highways as adopted in the constitutional convention . . . September, 1944. 6, [1] p.—The new article on local government as pending in the constitutional convention . . . June, 1944. 8 p.—The new article on state finance as pending in the constitutional convention . . . 7, [1] p.—The new article on taxation as adopted in the constitutional convention . . . 8 p. [1] p.—The new article on the Judicial Department as pending in the constitutional convention . . . 8 p.

[Mo 32]
Missouri. Constitutional Convention, 1943-1944.
    Proposal no. 1-[375] in the 1943 constitutional convention of Missouri. [Jefferson City, 1943]
    377 nos.

    ———. Index by subject matter, by committee reference, by author, and numerically. Also a chart showing the number of proposals in each committee. Proposals 1 to 375. Prepared by the office of the secretary. [Jefferson City, 1943]
    27 p.

[Mo 33]
Missouri. Constitutional Convention, 1943-1944.
Report of Committee no. 22 on information, submission, and address to the people . . . [Jefferson City, 1944]
13 p.

[Mo 34]
Missouri. Constitutional Convention, 1943-1944.
Rules, committees, members and officers, 1943. Prepared by the office of the secretary. [Jefferson City, 1943]
65 p.

On cover: Manual.

[Mo 35]
Missouri. Constitutional Convention, 1943-1944.
File no. 1-21 in the 1943-1944 constitutional convention of Missouri. [Jefferson City, 1944]
21 nos. in 1 v.

Caption title.
Some of the numbers have title: "Engrossed file."
Some of the files issued in various numbers.

[Mo 36]
Missouri. Constitution.
The constitution of the state of Missouri, adopted by the people on February 27, 1945, with annotations and appendix comparing the provisions therein with the provisions in the constitution of 1875, as amended and in force on that date. Compiled and edited by Lester G. Seacat, member of the staff of the Committee on Legislative Research. [Jefferson City] 1945.
247 p. (Missouri. General Assembly. Committee on Legislative Research. Report no. 5)

[Mo 37]
Missouri. Constitution.

Constitution, state of Missouri, 1945, revised 1969. Adopted by vote of the people February 27, 1945. Became effective March 30, 1945. Includes amendments adopted November 2, 1948, November 7, 1950, November 4, 1952, January 24, 1956, November 8, 1960, March 6, 1962, August 17, 1965, January 14, 1965, November 8, 1966, August 6, 1968, November 5, 1968. Published by James C. Kirkpatrick, secretary of state. [Jefferson City, 1969?]

244 p.

Montana

[Mon 1]
Montana Historical Society.
Constitutional conventions of Montana. [List of members . . .
1866, 1884, 1889]

(In its Contributions . . . 1896. v. 2, p. 394-398)

[Mon 2]
Montana (Ter.) Constitutional Convention, 1884.
Constitution of the state of Montana, as adopted by the constitutional convention of the territory of Montana, at the session
thereof begun . . . January 14 . . . and concluded . . . February 9
. . . 1884, to which is appended an address to the electors of the
territory of Montana, prepared by direction of the convention.
Published by authority. Helena, 1884.
40, 8 p.

This constitution was not ratified.

[Mon 3]
Montana (Ter.) Constitutional Convention, 1889.
Proceedings and debates of the constitutional convention, held
in the city of Helena, Montana, July 4, 1889, August 17, 1889.
Helena, 1921.
7 p. 1., [3]-974, xlii p., front., ports.

[Mon 4]
Montana (Ter.) Constitutional Convention, 1889.
   Constitution of the state of Montana as adopted by the constitutional convention held at Helena, Montana, July 4, A. D. 1889, and ending August 17, A. D. 1889. And also an address to the people. Helena [1889?]
   76 p.

[Mon 5]
Montana. Constitution.
   Supplementary pamphlet to the constitution of Montana, containing amendments voted by the people of Montana 1928-1942, inclusive. [Helena] 1942.
   7 p.

[Mon 6]
Montana. Constitution.
   Constitution of the state of Montana . . . [Helena, 1946]
   75 p.

   Caption title.

Nebraska

Nebraska (Ter.) Constitutional Convention, 1864.

(*See* Nebraska. Constitutional convention, 1871 [Neb 2].
Official report of the debates and proceedings . . . York [1913]
v. 3)

[Neb 1]
Nebraska (Ter.) Constitution.
Constitution of the state of Nebraska. [n. p., 1866?]
p. [13]-27.

Caption title.

[Neb 2]
Nebraska. Constitutional Convention, 1871.
Official report of the debates and proceedings in the Nebraska
constitutional convention assembled in Lincoln, June thirteenth,
1871, from the original shorthand notes of John T. Bell, John
Hall, Dan Brown, and John Gray. Prepared for printer (1871) by
Guy A. Brown, clerk of the Supreme Court of Nebraska. Revised,
edited, and indexed for publication (1905-[1907]) by Addison E.
Sheldon . . . Published by the Nebraska State Historical Society
pursuant to resolution of the twenty-ninth session of the Nebraska legislature . . . York [1906-13]
3 v. ports., fold. tables. (Nebraska State Historical Society.
Publications, v. 11-13, series II, v. vi-viii)

[Neb 2, cont.]

V. 3 is without imprint and has title: Official report of the debates and proceedings in the Nebraska constitutional convention . . . concluded; the journals of the convention of 1875; a history of the attempt to form a state organization in 1860, of the abortive constitutional convention of 1864, of the formation and adoption of the constitution of 1866, and of the conventions of 1871 and 1875 . . . revised and edited by Albert Watkins.

Nebraska. Constitutional Convention, 1875.
Journal.

(*See* Nebraska. Constitutional convention, 1871 [Neb 2]. Official report of the debates and proceedings . . . York [1913] v. 3)

[Neb 3]
Nebraska. Constitution.
. . . Nebraska constitutions of 1866, 1871, and 1875 and proposed amendments submitted to the people September 21, 1920. Arranged in parallel columns, with critical notes and comparisons with constitutions of other states. A joint publication of Nebraska Legislative Reference Bureau and Nebraska State Historical Society . . . Lincoln, 1920.

207, 7 p. ([Nebraska Legislative Reference Bureau] Bulletin, no. 13)

Nebraska history and political science series.

[Neb 4]
Nebraska. Constitution.
The constitution of the state of Nebraska, with judicial interpretations, prepared and edited by the Preliminary Survey Committee of the Constitutional Convention, for the constitutional convention, 1919 . . . [n. p.] 1919.

130 p.

Interleaved copy.
Appendix: ". . . copies of all amendments to the Constitution which have been defeated at a general election or superseded by subsequent amendments," p. 101-122.

[Neb 5]
Nebraska. Secretary of State.
. . . State constitutional convention . . . Official roster of delegates and state officers . . . [convention to be convened . . . on
second day of December, 1919 . . . [n. p.] 1919.
6 p. (folder)

[Neb 6]
Nebraska. Constitutional Convention, 1919-1920.
Journal of the Nebraska constitutional convention. Convened in
Lincoln, December 2, 1919. Compiled under authority of the con-
vention by Clyde H. Barnard, secretary . . . [Lincoln, 1921?]
2 v. (xii, 2977 p.) ports., tables, forms.

Running title: Proceedings of the Nebraska constitutional convention, 1919-1920.

[Neb 7]
——. Subject index to the proceedings. Compiled by William H.
Carlson. Lincoln, 1925.
15 p.

[Neb 8]
Nebraska. Constitutional Convention, 1919-1920.
An address to the people of Nebraska, pertaining to the proposed amendments to the constitution of the state, as adopted by
the constitutional convention, 1919-1920. To be submitted at a
special election to be held Tuesday, September 21, 1920 . . . [n. p.,
1920]
16 p.

[Neb 9]
Nebraska. Constitutional Convention, 1919-1920.
Proposed amendments to the constitution of the state of
Nebraska as adopted by the constitutional convention, 1919-
1920, with explanatory statements and sample ballot to be sub-
mitted to the people at a special election to be held Tuesday,
September 21, 1920. [n. p., 1920?]
40, [8] p.

[Neb 10]
Nebraska. Constitution.
Constitution of the state of Nebraska. Distributed by Frank
Marsh, secretary of state. Lincoln, 1966.
50 p.

Cover title.

Nevada

[Nev 1]
Nevada (Ter.) Constitutional Convention, 1864.
    Official report of the debates and proceedings in the constitutional convention of the state of Nevada, assembled at Carson City, July 4, 1864, to form a constitution and state government. A. J. Marsh, official reporter. San Francisco, 1866.
    xvi, 943 p.

    Contents:—Note by the reporter.—Organic act of the territory of Nevada, approved March 2, 1861.—Enabling act and act amendatory thereof, approved March 21 and May 21, 1864.—Proclamation of the governor of the territory calling the convention, May 2, 1864.—Abstract of votes upon the constitution.—Proclamation of the President admitting the state of Nevada into the Union.—Homographic chart of the convention.—Constitution of the state of Nevada.—Indices.—Errata.

[Nev 2]
Nevada (Ter.) Constitutional Convention, 1864.
    Constitution of the state of Nevada, together with the resolutions and ordinances as passed by the state constitutional convention, Thursday, July 28, 1864. Carson City, 1865.
    42 p., chart.

[Nev 3]
Nevada. Constitution.
. . . The constitution of the state of Nevada, its formation and interpretation, by . . . A. J. Maestretti and Charles Roger Hicks . . . 2d rev. ed. Reno [1947]
125 p. (University of Nevada bulletin, v. 61, no. 7)

As amended up to 1947.
Bibliography: p. [111]-112.

[Nev 4]
Nevada. Constitution.
The constitution of the state of Nevada; a commentary by Don W. Driggs. Carson City, 1961.
86 p. (Nevada studies in history and political science, no. 1)

Bibliographical footnotes.

New Hampshire

[NH 1]
New Hampshire (Colony) Fifth Provincial Congress, 1775-1776.
[Journal]

(In New Hampshire. [Provincial and state papers] Concord
[etc.] 1867-   v. 7, p. 704; v. 8, p. [1]-4)

The Congress assembled at Exeter on December 21, 1775, and
completed the framing of a constitution on January 5, 1776.

[NH 2]
New Hampshire. Constitution.
Constitution of New Hampshire—1776.

(In Thorpe, Francis Newton, comp. The federal and state constitutions, colonial charters, and other organic laws of the states,
territories, and colonies now or heretofore forming the United
States of America. Washington, 1909. v. 4, p. 2451-2453)

[NH 3-NH 6]
New Hampshire. Constitutional Conventions, 1778-1779, 1781-
1783
Constitutional conventions in New Hampshire, 1778-1783; with
the constitution established in 1784.

(In New Hampshire. [Provincial and state papers] Concord
[etc.] 1867-   v. 9. Appendix: p. [831]-919)

[NH 3-NH 6, cont.]
Contents:—Notes by the editor, p. [833]-834.—List of delegates, p. 834-837.—The constitution proposed in 1779, p. 837-842.—The second constitutional convention, p. 842-844.—An address of the convention, p. 845-852.—Proposed constitution of 1781, p. 852-877.—Second address of the convention, p. 877-882.—A constitution or form of government, p. 883-919.

[NH 7]
New Hampshire. Constitutional Convention, 1791-1792.
Journal of the convention which assembled in Concord, to revise the constitution of New Hampshire, 1791-1792. Pamphlet edition, printed by order, for use of the convention assembled in Concord for revision of said constitution, in December, 1876. Copied from the original journal and edited by Nathaniel Bouton. Concord, 1876.
p. [23]-198.

Pages in this pamphlet correspond with those in v. 10 of provincial and state papers.
Constitution as agreed and amended: p. [169]-196.

[NH 8]
New Hampshire. Constitutional Convention, 1850-1851.
Proceedings and debates (as reported in the Daily Patriot) [Concord?] 1850-1851.
36 issues (November 7, 1850-January 4, 1851)

[NH 9]
New Hampshire. Constitutional Convention, 1850-1851.
Rules of the constitutional convention of the state of New Hampshire, with a list of its officers and members, their places of residence, occupations, ages and boarding places, and the number of their seats; to which are added the constitution òf New Hampshire and the constitution of the United States. Concord, 1850.
78 p.

[NH 10]
New Hampshire. Constitution.
The amended constitution of the state of New Hampshire, with the resolutions for submitting the amendments to the people. Concord, 1851.
16 p.

[NH 11]
New Hampshire. Constitutional Convention, 1876.
Journal of the constitutional convention of the state of New Hampshire, December, 1876. Concord, 1877.
280 p.

[NH 12]
New Hampshire. Constitutional Convention, 1876.
Vote on constitutional amendments, 1877. Manchester, 1885.
27 p.

Proclamation by Governor B. F. Prescott, at end.

[NH 13]
New Hampshire. Constitution.
The constitution of New Hampshire as amended by the constitutional convention held at Concord on the first Wednesday of December, A. D. 1876, with the several questions involving the amendments proposed as submitted by the convention to the vote of the people. Concord, 1877.
31 p.

[NH 14]
New Hampshire. Constitutional Convention, 1889.
Journal of the constitutional convention of the state of New Hampshire, January, 1889. Manchester, 1889.
308 p.

[NH 15]
New Hampshire. Constitution.
The constitution of New Hampshire as amended by the con-

[NH 15, cont.]
stitutional convention held at Concord on the first Wednesday
of January, A. D. 1889, with the several questions involving
the amendments proposed as submitted by the convention to
the vote of the people. Manchester, 1889.
    31 p.

[NH 16]
New Hampshire. Constitutional Convention, 1902.
    Convention to revise the constitution, December, 1902.
Concord, 1903.
    949 p.

    Contents:—Journal.—Appendices: A. Tables and information
ordered printed by vote of the convention. B. Tabulation of
votes. Proclamation by His Excellency, Governor N. J.
Bachelder. Constitution as amended.

[NH 17]
Colby, James Fairbanks, comp.
    Manual of the constitution of the state of New Hampshire.
Compiled from official sources and edited with sketch of the
constitutions of the state, the basis of representation, and
appendix. Concord, 1902.
    318 p.

[NH 18]
New Hampshire. Constitutional Convention, 1912.
    Convention to revise the constitution, June, 1912. Manchester,
1912.
    703 p.

    Appendix: Pamphlet issued by Secretary of State Edward N.
Pearson, under resolution of the convention—Tabulation of vote
of the people upon the several amendments.—Proclamation of His
Excellency, Governor Robert P. Bass.—The amended constitution.

[NH 19]
Colby, James Fairbanks, comp.
Manual of the constitution of the state of New Hampshire. Compiled from official sources and edited, with sketch of the constitutions of the state, the basis of representation, and appendix. Concord, 1912.
349 p., folded chart.

[NH 20]
New Hampshire. Constitutional Convention, 1918-1923.
Convention to revise the constitution, June 5, 1918, January 13, 1920, January 28, 1921. Manchester, 1921.
147, 493 p.

Convention to revise the constitution, January 20, 1920. Manchester, 1920, has separate title page.

[NH 21]
New Hampshire. Constitutional Convention, 1918-1923.
Convention to revise the constitution. Special session. February, 1923. Concord, 1923.
44, [2] p.

[NH 22]
New Hampshire. Constitutional Convention, 1918-1923.
Manual of the constitutional convention of 1918. Convened at the State House at Concord, June 5, 1918. [Concord, 1918]
299 p., plates.

[NH 23]
New Hampshire. Constitution.
The constitution of the state of New Hampshire. [Established October 31, 1783, to take effect June 2, 1784, as subsequently amended and in force January 1, 1929.] Concord [1929]
46 p.

[NH 24]
New Hampshire. Constitutional Convention, 1930.
Convention to revise the constitution, June, 1930. Manchester, 1930.
217 p.

[NH 25]
New Hampshire. Constitution.
The constitution of the state of New Hampshire. [Established October 31, 1783, to take effect June 2, 1784, as subsequently amended and in force January 1, 1935.] Concord [1935]
46 p.

[NH 26]
New Hampshire. Constitutional Convention, 1938-1941.
Convention to revise the constitution, May, 1938. Manchester [1938]
372 p.

[NH 27]
New Hampshire. Constitution.
Amendments adopted by the convention to revise the constitution, in session May 11 to June 1, 1938. [Concord? 1938?]
[4] p.

[NH 28]
New Hampshire. Constitutional Convention, 1938-1941.
Convention to revise the constitution, September, 1941. Manchester [1941]
131 p.

[NH 29]
New Hampshire. Constitutional Convention, 1948.
Convention to revise the constitution, May, 1948. [Manchester, 1948?]
337 p.

[NH 30]
New Hampshire. Constitution.
Constitution of the state of New Hampshire established October 31, 1783, to take effect June 2, 1784, as subsequently amended and in force January 1, 1950.

(In New Hampshire register, state yearbook and legislative manual, 1957. Portland, Me., 1957. p. 69-82)

[NH 31]
New Hampshire. Constitutional Convention, 1956-1959.
Convention to revise the constitution. May, 1956. [Manchester, 1957?]
277 p.

[NH 32]
New Hampshire. Constitutional Convention, 1956-1959.
Convention to revise the constitution; reconvened session, December, 1959. [Peterborough, 1960?]
145 p.

[NH 33]
New Hampshire. Constitutional Convention, 1956-1959.
Voters' guide to proposed amendments to constitution of state of New Hampshire to appear on a special ballot at election on November 8, 1960. Recommended by the 14th constitutional convention at its reconvened session in December, 1959. [Manchester, 1960]
[6] p. (folder)

[NH 34]
New Hampshire. Constitution.
The constitution of the state of New Hampshire established October 31, 1783 to take effect June 2, 1784, as subsequently amended and in force November, 1958. Concord [1958?]
44 p.

New Jersey

[NJ 1]
New Jersey (Colony) Convention, 1776.

Journal of the votes and proceedings of the convention of New Jersey, begun at Burlington the 10th of June 1776, and thence continued by adjournment at Trenton and New-Brunswick to the 21st of August following. To which is annexed sundry ordinances, and the constitution. Burlington, 1776.

150 p.

[NJ 2]
New Jersey. Governor.

Proclamation of the governor and act calling a convention.
[n.p., 1844]

[2], 8 p.

[NJ 3]
New Jersey. Constitutional Convention, 1844.

Journal of the proceedings of the convention to form a constitution for the government of the state of New Jersey: begun at Trenton on the fourteenth day of May, 1844, and continued to the twenty-ninth day of June, A. D. 1844. Trenton, 1844.

297 p.

Includes proclamation by Daniel Haines, governor of the state of New Jersey.

[NJ 4]
New Jersey. Constitutional Convention, 1844.
Proceedings of the New Jersey state constitutional convention of 1844. Compiled and edited by the New Jersey Writers Project ... with an introduction by John Bebout. [Trenton? 1942?] cxx, 655 p.

Constitution agreed upon: p. [613]-633.

[NJ 5]
New Jersey. Commission on Constitutional Amendments.
Special message of His Excellency Geo. C. Ludlow, governor of New Jersey, presenting to the legislature the report of the Commission on Constitutional Amendments, together with the Assembly bill introduced January 11, 1882. [Trenton, 1882] 46 p.

At head of title: Document no. 2.

[NJ 6]
New Jersey. Laws, statutes, etc.
Proposed amendments to the constitution of New Jersey, 1927. Trenton [1927] 15 p.

"Chapter 323, P. L. 1927."

[NJ 7]
New Jersey. Constitution.
Constitution of the state of New Jersey. [Trenton] 1941. 34 p.

[NJ 8]
New Jersey. Commission on Revision of the Constitution.
Report of the Commission on Revision of the New Jersey Constitution appointed pursuant to Laws of 1941, joint resolution no. 2. Submitted to the governor, the legislature, and the people of New Jersey, May, 1942. Trenton, [1942] 59 p.

[NJ 9]
New Jersey. Legislature. Joint Committee to Ascertain the Senti-
ments of the People of the State as to the Various Proposals
and Recommendations for Change in the New Jersey Constitution.

Record of proceedings before the Joint Committee of the New
Jersey Legislature constituted under Senate concurrent resolution
no. 19, entitled "A concurrent resolution creating a joint legislative committee to ascertain the sentiment of the people of the
State as to the various proposals and recommendations for change
in the New Jersey Constitution made by the Commission on Revision of the New Jersey Constitution and to report thereon to
the Legislature," adopted June 15, 1942 . . . [Trenton? 1943]
    1124, 8 p.

[NJ 10]
New Jersey, Governor, 1941-1944 (Charles Edison)
    A new constitution for New Jersey. Addresses by Charles
Edison. [n. p., n. d.]
    55 p.

[NJ 11]
New Jersey. Governor, 1941-1944 (Charles Edison)
    Speeches on the constitution of New Jersey, by Governor
Charles Edison. [n. p., 1943]
    29 p.

[NJ 12]
New Jersey. Legislature. Joint Committee to Formulate a Draft
of a Proposed Revised Constitution.

Proposed revised constitution (1944) pending before Joint
Legislative Committee to Formulate a Draft of a Proposed Re-
vised Constitution for the State of New Jersey constituted under
Senate concurrent resolution no. 1, adopted January 11, 1944
. . . Trenton [1944]
    26 p.

[NJ 13]
New Jersey. Constitution.
Proposed constitutional revision of 1944. Chart showing the principal changes proposed in the 1942 report of the Hendrickson Commission, and the action taken upon them by the legislature, indicating where the changes were adopted or rejected in the preliminary draft adopted by the legislature prior to the public hearings, and where such action was changed in the final draft which was submitted to the people at the November, 1944 election. Compiled by Leslie H. Jamouneau. [Trenton? 1944]
10 numb. l.

Caption title.

[NJ 14]
New Jersey. Constitutional Convention, 1947.
Constitutional convention of 1947, held at Rutgers University, the State University of New Jersey, New Brunswick, New Jersey. [Proceedings. Trenton, 1949-1953]
5 v.

[NJ 15]
New Jersey. Constitutional Convention, 1947.
Official rules adopted by the constitutional convention with list of delegates and committees . . . Trenton, 1947.
36 p.

[NJ 16]
New Jersey. Constitutional Convention, 1947.
Biographies of delegates. [New Brunswick? 1947]
[88] numb. l.

[NJ 17]
New Jersey. Governor's Committee on Preparatory Research for the New Jersey Constitutional Convention.
[Series of monographs. Trenton?] 1947.
2 v.

[NJ 18]
New Jersey. Constitutional Convention, 1947.
[What the proposed new state constitution means to you] a report to the people of New Jersey by their elected delegates to the constitutional convention. New Brunswick, 1947.
7 p.

[NJ 19]
New Jersey. Constitution.
A new constitution for the state, agreed upon by the delegates of the people of New Jersey in convention, at Rutgers University . . . on September 10, 1947. To be submitted to the people for their adoption or rejection, as a whole, at the general election on November 4, 1947. [n. p., 1947]
30 p.

[NJ 20]
New Jersey. Constitution.
State constitution.

(In New Jersey. Legislature. Manual of the legislature of New Jersey, one hundred and eighty-fourth session, 1960. Trenton, 1960. p. 55-88)

New Mexico

[NM 1]
New Mexico (Ter.) Convention, 1849.

Journal and proceedings of a convention of delegates elected by the people of New Mexico, held at Santa Fe on the 24th of September, 1849, presenting a plan for civil government of said territory of New Mexico, and asking the action of Congress thereon. February 25, 1850. Referred to the Committee on Territories and ordered to be printed. [Washington? 1850?]

13 p. ([U. S.] 31st Cong., 1st sess. House. Misc. Doc. 39)

Caption title.

[NM 3]
New Mexico (Ter.) Constitution.

Constitution of the state of New Mexico, 1850. [Santa Fe, 1965]

46 p., map. (Historians' editions)

This constitution never went into effect.

[NM 4]
New Mexico (Ter.) Laws, statutes, etc.

. . . Council bill no. 35, providing for the holding of a constitutional convention. Introduced by Senator Prichard . . . and passed. Law by limitation, February 28, 1889. Santa Fe, 1889.

1 p. l., 5 p.

At head of title: 28th Legislative Assembly. Territory of New Mexico.

[NM 5]
New Mexico (Ter.) Governor.
  Proclamation [issued June 24, 1889, giving notice of a consti-
tutional convention in Santa Fe, September 3, 1889. Santa Fe,
1889]
  Broadside.

[NM 6]
New Mexico (Ter.) Constitutional Convention, 1889.
  The constitution of the state of New Mexico adopted by the
constitutional convention, held at Santa Fe, N. M., September
3-21, 1889; amended August 18-20, 1890; and address to the
people by a committee of the convention.
  56 p.

  Cover title.

[NM 7]
New Mexico (Ter.) Constitutional Convention, 1889.
  Memorial of William C. Hazeldine [!] in behalf of the committee
appointed by the constitutional convention of New Mexico, to
present the constitution framed by said convention to Congress,
asking the passage of an enabling act for the admission of New
Mexico under such constitution when ratified by the people.
[Washington?] 1890.
  22 p. ([U. S.] 51st Cong., 1st sess. Senate. Misc. Doc. 121)

  Caption title.

[NM 8]
New Mexico (Ter.) Constitutional Convention, 1910.
  Rules of the constitutional convention, formed for the purpose
of framing a constitution for the proposed state of New Mexico,
1910. Santa Fe, 1910.
  15 p.

  Cover title.

[NM 9]
New Mexico (Ter.) Constitutional Convention, 1910.
Proceedings of the constitutional convention of the proposed state of New Mexico, held at Santa Fe, New Mexico, October 3, 1910, to November 21, 1910.
292 p.

[NM 10]
New Mexico (Ter.) Constitution.
The constitution of the state of New Mexico, adopted by the constitutional convention, held at Santa Fe, N. M., from October 3 to November 21, 1910. [Santa Fe? 1910]
41 p.

Caption title
Rejected by the 3d session of the 61st Congress.

[NM 11]
New Mexico. Constitution.
Annotated constitution and enabling act of the state of New Mexico, comprising the enabling act for the territory of New Mexico, approved June 20, 1910; the constitution of the state of New Mexico, adopted by the constitutional convention, November 21, 1910, ratified by the people at the election therefor, January 21, 1911; the act of Congress for admission to statehood, approved August 21, 1911. Annotated and indexed; compiler . . . Arthur G. Whittier . . . Santa Fe [1911]
174 p., fold. facsim.

[NM 12]
New Mexico. Constitution.
The constitution of the state of New Mexico, as adopted January 21, 1911, and as subsequently amended by the people in general and special elections, 1912 through 1958 . . . January, 1959. [Portales, 1959]
80 p.

New York

[NY 4]
New York (State) Constitution.
   Constitution of New York—1777.

   (In Thorpe, Francis Newton, comp. The federal and state constitutions, colonial charters, and other organic laws of the states, territories, and colonies now or heretofore forming the United States of America. Washington, 1909. v. 5, p. 2623-2638)

[NY 5]
New York (State) Constitutional Convention, 1801.
   Journal of the convention of the state of New-York. Began and held at the city of Albany, on the 13th day of October, 1801. Albany, 1801.
   42 p., mounted port. laid in.

[NY 6]
New York (State) Constitution.
   Amendments to the constitution of 1777.
   (In convention of delegates, Albany, October 27, 1801)

   (In Thorpe, Francis Newton, comp. The federal and state constitutions, colonial charters, and other organic laws of the states, territories, and colonies now or heretofore forming the United States of America. Washington, 1909. v. 5, p. 2638-2639)

[NY 7]
New York (State) Constitutional Convention, 1821.
   Journal of the convention of the state of New York. Begun and held at the Capitol in the city of Albany, on the twenty-eighth day of August, 1821. Albany, 1821.
   564, xii p.

[NY 8]
New York (State) Constitutional Convention, 1821.
   Reports of the proceedings and debates of the convention of

[NY 8, cont.]
1821, assembled for the purpose of amending the constitution of
the state of New York: containing all the official documents, relating to the subject, and other valuable matter. By Nathaniel H.
Carter and William L. Stone, reporters: and Marcus T. C. Gould,
stenographer. Albany, 1821.
    viii, [9]-703 p.

[NY 10]
New York (State) Constitution.
    Constitution of the state of New York, as amended. Albany,
1821.
    4, 24 p.

    Contains address of the delegates in convention to their con-
stituents and resolutions.

[NY 11]
Convention of Friends of Constitutional Reform, Utica, 1837.
    The address, and draft of a proposed constitution, submitted
to the people of the state of New-York, by a Convention of
Friends of Constitutional Reform, held at Utica, September,
1837. New York, 1837.
    4, 8 p.

    Signed at end of address: Robert Townsend, Jr., pres. [of the
convention]

[NY 12]
New York (State) Constitution.
    Amendments to the constitution of 1821 [ratified 1826, 1833,
1835, 1839, and 1845]

    (In Thorpe, Francis Newton, comp. The federal and state con-
stitutions, colonial charters, and other organic laws of the states,
territories, and colonies now or heretofore forming the United
States of America. Washington, 1909. v. 5, p. 2651-2653)

[NY 13]
New York (State) Constitutional Convention, 1846.
Journal of the convention of the state of New-York, begun and held at the Capitol in the city of Albany, on the first day of June, 1846. Albany, 1846.
1648 p.

[NY 14]
New York (State) Constitutional Convention, 1846.
Report of the debates and proceedings of the convention for the revision of the constitution of the state of New York, 1846. Reported by William G. Bishop and William H. Attree. Albany, 1846.
1143 p., diagr.

Constitution as amended: p. [7]-16.

[NY 15]
New York (State) Constitutional Convention, 1846.
Documents of the convention of the state of New-York, 1846. Albany, 1846.
2 v.

[NY 16]
New York (State) Constitutional Convention, 1846.
Manual for the use of the convention to revise the constitution of the state of New York, convened at Albany, June 1, 1846. New York, 1846.
371 p.

[NY 17]
New York (State) Constitution.
The constitution of the state of New-York, adopted November 3, 1846; together with marginal notes and a copious index. [Prepared by I. R. Elwood, Esq., late clerk of the Senate] Albany, 1849.
55 p.

[NY 18]
New York (State) Constitution.
Amendments to the constitution of 1846.

(In Thorpe, Francis Newton, comp. The federal and state constitutions, colonial charters, and other organic laws of the states, territories, and colonies now or heretofore forming the United States of America. Washington, 1909. v. 5, p. 2675-2692)

[NY 19]
New York (State) Constitutional Convention, 1867-1868.
Journal of the convention of the state of New York, begun and held at the Capitol, in the city of Albany, on the 4th day of June, 1867. Albany, 1867.
1547 p.

[NY 20]
New York (State) Constitutional Convention, 1867-1868.
Report of the proceedings and debates of the convention for the revision of the constitution of the state of New York, 1867-1868. Reported by E. F. Underhill. Albany, 1868.
5 v. ([19]-3971, ccxlvii p.)

[NY 21]
New York (State) Constitutional Convention, 1867-1868.
Documents of the convention of the state of New York, 1867-1868. [No. 1 to 185] Albany, 1868.
5 v., folded maps.

Includes the constitution as revised, amended, and adopted by the convention.

[NY 22]
New York (State) Constitutional Convention, 1867-1868.
New York convention manual, prepared in pursuance of chapters 194 and 458, of the laws of 1867, under the direction of Francis C. Barlow, secretary of state, Thomas Hillhouse, comptroller, and John H. Martindale, attorney general. By Franklin B. Hough. Albany, 1867.
2 v., folded diagr.

[NY 23]
New York (State) Constitution.
The amended constitution of the state of New York, adopted by the convention of 1867-1868, together with the manner and form of submission and an address to the people. Albany, 1868.
83 p.

The constitution was rejected, except for the new judiciary article VI, which was adopted by the people and became an amendment to the 1846 constitution.

[NY 24]
New York (State) Constitution.
[Article VI, ratified 1869]

(In Poore, Ben. Perley, comp. The federal and state constitu-)n tions, colonial charters, and other organic laws of the United States. Washington, 1877. v. 2, p. 1368-1372)

[NY 25]
New York (State) Constitutional Commission, 1872-1873.
Journal of the Constitutional Commission of the state of New York. Begun and held in the Common Council chamber, in the city of Albany, on the 4th day of December, 1872-1873.
1 v. (various pagings)

Appendix no. 3: The constitution as amended . . . in comparison with the existing constitution.

[NY 26]
New York (State) Constitution.
Constitution of the state of New-York as amended at the late election. New York, 1874.
49 p.

[NY 27]
New York (State) Constitution.
Constitution of the state of New York. Annotated to and including the year 1889. Albany, 1890.
p. [45]-158.

[NY 28]
New York (State) Constitutional Commission, 1890-1891.
Journal. [Albany, 1891]
125 p.

Caption title.
The commission, meeting at Albany June 3, 1890, was authorized to prepare amendments to the judiciary article of the constitution, but its report, submitted on March 4, 1891, was so late that the legislature could not consider it, and no action was taken. Its proposals, however, were later adopted by the convention of 1894. Cf. E. H. Breuer. Constitutional developments in New York 1777-1958. 1958.

[NY 29]
New York (State) Constitutional Commission, 1890-1891.
[Report of committees for judiciary. Albany? 1890]
[33] numb. l.

[NY 30]
New York (State) Constitutional Convention, 1894.
Journal of the constitutional convention of the state of New York. 1894. Revised and indexed . . . Albany, 1895.
1001 p.

[NY 31]
New York (State) Constitutional Convention, 1894.
Revised record of the constitutional convention of the state of New York, May 8, 1894, to September 29, 1894. Revised and indexed by Hon. William H. Steele . . . Published under direction of Hon. Charles E. Fitch . . . Albany, 1900.
5 v.

[NY 32]
New York (State) Constitutional Convention, 1894.
[Documents. Albany? 1894]
2 v.

[NY 32, cont.]

". . . Proposed revised Constitution as adopted by the Constitutional Convention, at the city of Albany, September 28, 1894": 129 p. at end of v. 2.

[NY 33]
New York (State) Constitutional Convention, 1894.

The convention manual of procedure, forms and rules for the regulation of business in the sixth New York state constitutional convention, 1894. Albany, 1894.

2 pts. in 10 v.

Part 1: v. 1-3; part 2: v. 1-7.

[NY 34]
New York (State) Constitution.

The proposed constitution of the state of New York, together with the addresses of the majority and minority delegates. Brooklyn, 1894.

(In Brooklyn Eagle Library, v. 1, no. 1, October, 1894, p. 1-30)

[NY 35]
New York (State) Constitution.

New York state constitution annotated . . . Prepared under the direction of the New York State Library. [Albany] 1915.

1 v. (various pagings)

Pt. 1.—Text in force April 6, 1915, with notes. Pt. 2.—Amendments adopted and proposed, 1895-1914.

[NY 36]
New York (State) Constitutional Convention, 1915.

Journal of the constitutional convention of the state of New York, 1915, begun and held at the Capitol in the city of Albany on Tuesday the sixth day of April. Albany, 1915.

1018 p.

[NY 37]
New York (State) Constitutional Convention, 1915.
Revised record of the constitutional convention of the state of New York, April sixth to September tenth, 1915 . . . Albany, 1916.
4 v. (4510 p.)

[NY 38]
New York (State) Constitutional Convention, 1915.
Documents of the constitutional convention of the state of New York, 1915, begun and held at the Capitol in the city of Albany on Tuesday the sixth day of April. Albany, 1915.
[724] p.

[NY 39]
New York (State) Constitutional Convention, 1915.
Rules of the 1915 constitutional convention; reprinted. [New York, 1915?]
36 p.

[NY 40]
New York (State) Constitutional Convention, 1915.
The convention manual of procedure, forms and rules for the regulation of business in the seventh New York state constitutional convention, 1915. Albany, 1915.
400 p., facsims., maps, ports.

[NY 41]
New York (State) Constitutional Convention, 1915.
Directory of delegates, post office addresses, committee assignments, seat numbers, and other information. [Albany, 1915?]
22 p.

[NY 42]
New York (State) Constitution.
Proposed constitution of the state of New York as amended and

[NY 42, cont.]

revised, adopted by the convention September 10, 1915, with explanatory abstracts and form for submission to the voters, pursuant to chapter 668, Laws of 1915. Prepared under the direction of Francis M. Hugo, secretary of state. [Albany, 1915]
   80 p.

"Address to the people of the State of New York" (by Elihu Root): p. [71]-79. The amendments were rejected by the people.

[NY 43]

New York (State) Constitutional Convention, 1921.
   [Reports and proceedings]

   (In New York [State] Constitutional Convention Committee [Reports. Albany] 1938. v. 9, p. 428-732)

[NY 44]

New York (State) Constitutional Convention, 1921.
   Proposed amendments to judiciary article of state constitution. Explanatory statement of the recommendations made by the Judiciary Constitutional Convention of 1921, dated March 19, 1924.
[Albany? 1924?]
   37 p.

   Signed: William D. Guthrie, chairman, Executive Committee of Judiciary Convention of 1921.

   The proposed judiciary article was not adopted, but many changes suggested by this convention and the convention of 1915 were eventually incorporated in the revised judiciary article adopted in 1925. Cf. E. H. Breuer. Constitutional developments in New York 1777-1958. 1958.

[NY 45]

New York (State) Legislature. Joint Committee on Revision of the Constitution and Election Law.
   Report of the Joint Legislative Committee on Revision of the

[NY 45, cont.]

Constitution and the Election Law. Albany, 1933.

15 p. ([New York (State) Legislature] legislative document, 1933, no. 78)

[NY 46]
New York (State) Constitution.

The constitution of the state of New York as proposed by the constitutional convention, September 29, 1894, at Albany, N. Y., and adopted by the people of the state, November 6, 1894. As amended and in force January 1, 1938. [Albany, 1937?]

p. 85-235.

Caption title.

[NY 47]
New York (State) Constitutional Convention, 1938.

Journal of the constitutional convention of the state of New York, April fifth to August twenty-sixth, 1938. Albany, 1938.

[1190] p.

Contents.—Journal.—Appendix to journal. No. 1. Points of order. No. 2. Rules of the 1938 constitutional convention. No. 3. Documents of the constitutional convention of 1938.

[NY 48]
New York (State) Constitutional Convention, 1938.

Revised record of the constitutional convention of the state of New York, April fifth to August twenty-sixth, 1938 . . . Albany, 1938.

4 v. (3542 p.)

[NY 49]
New York (State) Constitutional Convention, 1938.

Proposed amendments of the constitutional convention of the state of New York, April fifth to August twenty-sixth, 1938 . . . Albany, 1938.

3 v.

Six of the convention's nine proposals were approved.

[NY 50]
New York (State) Constitution.
The constitution of the state of New York, as revised, with amendments adopted by the constitutional convention of 1938 and approved by vote of the people on November 8, 1938. As amended and in force January 1, 1939. Albany [1939]
254 p.

[NY 51]
New York (State) Temporary Commission on the Constitutional Convention.
Interim report, 1st-2d. [Albany] 1957.
17, 58 p. ([New York (State) Legislature] legislative document, 1957, no. 8, 57)

The commission was created in 1956 to prepare for a possible convention in 1959. It was terminated on February 1, 1958, as a result of the negative vote on the question of calling a convention at the November, 1957 election. Cf. E. H. Breuer. Constitutional developments in New York 1777-1958. 1958.

[NY 52]
New York (State) Temporary Commission on the Constitutional Convention.
Transcript of public hearing . . . New York, 1957.
4 v.

Hearings held June 4-5, 14-17, 1957.

[NY 53]
New York (State) Inter-law School Committee on Constitutional Simplification.
Report on the problem of simplification of the constitution. [Albany] 1958.
225 p. (Special Legislative Committee on the Revision and Simplification of the Constitution. Staff report no. 1)

[NY 53, cont.]

[New York (State) Legislature] legislative document, 1958, no. 57.

The committee was established by the Temporary State Commission on the Constitutional Convention in the spring of 1957 to study the implications of simplifying the constitution.

[NY 54]

New York (State) Temporary Commission on the Revision and Simplification of the Constitution.

First steps toward a modern constitution. New York, 1959.

104 p. ([New York (State) Legislature] legislative document, 1959, no. 58)

The commission, which was created in 1959 for a two-year period, succeeded a Special Legislative Committee appointed in 1958 to continue the studies begun by the Temporary Commission on the Constitutional Convention.

[NY 55]

New York (State) Constitution.

The constitution of the state of New York, as revised, with amendments adopted by the constitutional convention of 1938 and approved by vote of the people on November 8, 1938, as amended and in force January 1, 1960. [Albany, 1960]

267 p.

North Carolina

[NC 1]
Mecklenburg County, N. C.
   The Mecklenburgh resolutions—1775.

   (In Thorpe, Francis Newton, comp. The federal and state constitutions, colonial charters, and other organic laws of the states,
territories, and colonies now or heretofore forming the United
States of America. Washington, 1909. v. 5, p. 2786-2787)

   A set of resolves establishing a form of government, which were
adopted by a convention of delegates from Mecklenburg County
meeting in Charlotte on May 31, 1775. They followed the controversial Mecklenburg declaration of independence, alleged to
have been drawn up on May 20.

[NC 2]
North Carolina (Colony) Provincial Congress, November 12-
      December 23, 1776.
   The journal of the proceedings of the Provincial Congress of
North-Carolina, held at Halifax, the 12th day of November,
1776. Together with the declaration of rights, constitution, and
ordinances of Congress. Newbern, 1777.
   84 p.

[NC 3]
North Carolina. Convention, 1823.
The journal of a convention assembled at the city of Raleigh, on the 10th of November, 1823, to adopt such measures as were deemed necessary to procure an amendment to the constitution of North Carolina. Raleigh, 1823.
11 p.

[NC 4]
North Carolina. Convention, 1823.
Proposed new constitution of the state of North Carolina, as agreed upon by the convention assembled at Raleigh on the 10th of November, 1823; together with a copy of the present constitution. Raleigh, 1823.
15 p.

This constitution was not accepted.

[NC 5]
Address to the freemen of North Carolina on the subject of amending the state constitution, with the amendments reported to the legislature at the session of 1832-1833 by the committee appointed at a meeting held in Raleigh. Raleigh, 1833.
18 p.

[NC 6]
North Carolina. General Assembly. Joint Select Committee on Amending the Constitution.
Report of the Joint Select Committee on Amending the Constitution of the State of North Carolina. Raleigh [1833]
7 p.

At head of title: No. 12. Legislature of North Carolina, 1833. Report signed by Osmyn B. Irvine, chairman.

[NC 7]
North Carolina. Constitutional Convention, 1835.
Journal of the convention called by the freemen of North Carolina, to amend the constitution of the state, which assembled in the city of Raleigh, on the 4th of June, 1835, and continued in session until the 11th day of July thereafter. Raleigh, 1835.
106 p.

[NC 8]
North Carolina. Constitutional Convention, 1835.
Proceedings and debates of the convention of North Carolina, called to amend the constitution of the state, which assembled at Raleigh, June 4, 1835. To which are subjoined the convention act and the amendments to the constitution, together with the votes of the people. Raleigh, 1836.
424, [1], 6 p.

[NC 9]
North Carolina. Constitutional Convention, 1835.
Rules of order for the government of the convention assembled at Raleigh on Thursday, the 4th of June, 1835, to revise the constitution of the state of North Carolina. Raleigh, 1835.
7 p.

[NC 10]
North Carolina. Constitutional Convention, 1835.
Report [of the committee to whom was referred so much of the act entitled An act concerning a convention to amend the constitution of this state so as to reduce the number of members of the Senate. Raleigh, 1835]
3 p.

Caption title.

[NC 11]
North Carolina. Constitutional Convention, 1835.
Report [of the committee to whom was referred the report of

[NC 11, cont.]
the Committee of Twenty-Six, as amended by the convention,
for the purpose of framing an article in conformity thereto, to be
incorporated in the amended constitution. Raleigh, 1835]
   3 p.

Caption title.

[NC 12]
North Carolina. Constitutional Convention, 1835.
   [Report of the committee who were instructed by the convention to arrange the senatorial districts, and apportion the members
of the House of Commons among the several counties. Raleigh,
1835.]
   12 p.

Caption title.

[NC 13]
North Carolina. Constitutional Convention, 1835.
   Report; the committee, to whom was referred the 18th resolution, reported by the Committee of Thirteen . . . report . . .
articles as amendments of the constitution. [Raleigh, 1835]
   [1] p.

Caption title.

[NC 14]
North Carolina. Constitutional Convention, 1835.
   Reports [of the committee . . . to enquire . . . what amendments
were necessary to be made in the 5th and 7th articles of the constitution, in relation to the residence and qualifications of persons
voting for senators, and of persons eligible to the Senate . . . (and
other committees, on amendments to the constitution) Raleigh,
1835]
   4 p.

Caption title.

[NC 15]
North Carolina. Constitutional Convention, 1835.
Reports [of the committee to whom was referred the 14th resolution, reported by the Committee of Twenty-Six . . . and other committees, on amendments to the constitution. Raleigh, 1835

3 p.

Caption title.

[NC 16]
North Carolina. Constitution.
The constitution of North Carolina, adopted December 17, 1776; and the amendments thereto, submitted to the people by the convention which assembled at Raleigh, June 4, 1835; together with an ordinance for carrying the same into effect. Raleigh, 1835.

24 p.

[NC 17]
North Carolina. Constitution.
Amendments to the constitution of 1776 [ratified 1835]

(In Thorpe, Francis Newton, comp. The federal and state constitutions, colonial charters, and other organic laws of the states, territories, and colonies now or heretofore forming the United States of America. Washington, 1909. v. 5, p. 2794-2799)

[NC 18]
North Carolina. Convention, 1861-1862.
Journal of the convention of the people of North Carolina held on the 20th day of May, A. D. 1861. Raleigh, 1862.

4 v. in 1.

Convention passed ordinance of secession and revised the constitution.

[NC 19]
North Carolina. Convention, 1861-1862.
Ordinances of the state convention, published in pursuance of a resolution of the General Assembly. Ratified 11 February, 1863. Raleigh, 1863.
93, ii, ii, ii p.

[NC 20]
North Carolina. Constitutional Convention, 1865-1866.
Journal of the convention of the state of North-Carolina at its session of 1865. Raleigh, 1865.
94, iii p.

The convention met in Raleigh October 2-19, 1865, repealed the secession ordinance, and adopted an anti-slavery ordinance, which was ratified by the people.

[NC 21]
North Carolina. Constitutional Convention, 1865-1866.
Journal of the convention of the state of North-Carolina, at its adjourned session of 1866. Raleigh, 1866.
192, iii p.

The convention reassembled in May, 1866, and reconstructed the 1776 constitution, but this was rejected by the people.

[NC 22]
North Carolina. Constitutional Convention, 1865-1866.
Executive documents. Convention, session 1865. Constitution of North Carolina, with amendments, and ordinances and resolutions passed by the convention, session 1865. Raleigh, 1865.
1 v. (various pagings), 2 folded charts.

[NC 23]
North Carolina. Constitutional Convention, 1865-1866.
Ordinances and resolutions passed by the North Carolina state convention, second session, 1866. Raleigh. 1866.
57, 6, iii p.

[NC 24]
North Carolina. Constitutional Convention, 1865-1866.
   Rules of order. [Raleigh, 1865]
   5 p. (Doc. no. 2. sess. 1865)

   Caption title.

[NC 25]
North Carolina. Constitutional Convention, 1868.
   Journal of the constitutional convention of the state of North-
Carolina, at its session 1868. Raleigh, 1868.
   488, [1] p.

[NC 26]
North Carolina. Constitutional Convention, 1868.
   To the people of North Carolina. [n. p., 1868]
   46, 2 p.

   Contents.—Address. (Signed: Will B. Rodman and Geo. W.
Gahagan)—Constitution of North Carolina.—Ordinances.

[NC 27]
North Carolina. Constitutional Convention, 1868.
   Constitution of the state of North-Carolina, together with the
ordinances and resolutions of the constitutional convention, assembled in the city of Raleigh, January 14, 1868. Raleigh, 1868.
   129, iv p.

[NC 28]
North Carolina. Constitutional Convention, 1875.
   Journal of the constitutional convention of the state of North
Carolina, held in 1875. Raleigh, 1875.
   286, xx p.

[NC 29]
North Carolina. Constitutional Convention, 1875.
   Ordinances. [Raleigh? 1875?]
   30 p.

   Caption title.

[NC 30]
North Carolina. Constitution.
Amendments to the constitution of North Carolina, proposed by the constitutional convention of 1875, and the constitution as it will read as proposed to be amended. Prepared under ordinances of the convention, by Johnstone Jones, secretary of the convention, and John Reilly, state auditor . . . Raleigh, 1875.
70 p.

[NC 31]
North Carolina. Constitution.
The constitution of the state of North Carolina, annotated, by Henry G. Connor . . . and Joseph B. Cheshire, Jr. . . . Raleigh, 1911.
lxxx, 510 p.

[NC 32]
North Carolina. Commission on Constitutional Amendments.
Report of Commission on Constitutional Amendments to Governor Locke Craig. July 18, 1913. Raleigh, 1913.
15, [1] p.

"A bill to be entitled An act to amend the Constitution of the State of North Carolina": p. [7]-15.

[NC 33]
North Carolina. Commission on Constitutional Amendments.
Resolutions of the General Assembly creating the commission. Minutes of the sessions of the commission. Rules adopted by the commission. Raleigh, 1913.
89 p.

[NC 34]
North Carolina. Constitution.
Constitution of the state of North Carolina and copy of the act of the General Assembly entitled, An act to amend the constitution of the state of North Carolina (chapter 81, public laws, extra session of 1913). Issued from the office of the secretary

[NC 34, cont.]
of state, Raleigh, by authority of the General Assembly.
Raleigh, 1914.
47 p.

[NC 36]
North Carolina. Constitution.
The constitution of the state of North Carolina. Raleigh, 1927.
38 p.

[NC 37]
North Carolina. Constitution.
Proposed amendments to the constitution of North Carolina, to
be submitted at the election, November 6, 1928. Compiled by
H. M. London. Raleigh [1928]
7 p.

[NC 38]
North Carolina. Constitutional Commission.
The report of the North Carolina Constitutional Commission to
the governor and General Assembly. [Raleigh?] 1932.
50 p.

[NC 39]
North Carolina. Constitution.
The constitution of the state of North Carolina [as approved
by the General Assembly of 1933. Reproduced (from the public
laws of 1933) for the North Carolina Constitutional Commission
by Albert Coates. Chapel Hill? 1958?]
p. [547]-573.

Caption title.

[NC 40]
North Carolina. University. Institute of Government.
Commentaries on proposals in 1933 and 1935 for revision of

[NC 40, cont.]
the constitution of North Carolina. Compiled for the North
Carolina Constitutional Commission created by the 1957 General
Assembly, by Albert Coates, director, with the assistance of
Dexter Watts and William C. Frue, Jr. [Chapel Hill? 1958]
    88 p.

[NC 41]
North Carolina. Constitution.
    Amendments to the constitution of North Carolina proposed
by the General Assembly, 1937-1957: text and commentary.
Compiled for the North Carolina Constitutional Commission
created by the 1957 General Assembly, by Albert Coates, director,
with the assistance of L. Poindexter Watts and William C. Frue, Jr.
[Chapel Hill? 1958?]
    xvi, 95 p.

[NC 42]
North Carolina. Constitutional Commission.
    Report of the North Carolina Constitutional Commission to the
governor and members of the General Assembly of the state of
North Carolina. Raleigh, 1959.
    xvi, 146 p.

[NC 43]
North Carolina. Governor, 1954-1961 (Hodges)
    Special message of Governor Luther H. Hodges to the North
Carolina General Assembly, Hall of the House of Representatives, State Capitol, Raleigh, Thursday, March 12, 1959. [Raleigh,
1959]
    14 p.

    On the subject of the North Carolina constitution.

[NC 44]
**North Carolina. General Assembly. Senate. Committee on the
    Constitution.**
    Documents relating to the constitutional revision and court im-

[NC 44, cont.]
provement bills [considered by the North Carolina General Assembly of 1959. Compiled by John L. Sanders. Raleigh] 1959.
1 v. (various pagings)

[NC 45]
Sanders, John L.
A report on the convention of the people in North Carolina, 1776-1958; prepared for the North Carolina Constitutional Commission. [Chapel Hill, 1958]
41 numb. l. (North Carolina. University. Institute of Government. Special study, June, 1958)

[NC 46]
North Carolina. University. Institute of Government.
Article IV, Judicial Department, comparative texts. Prepared for the General Assembly of North Carolina by John L. Sanders, assistant director. Chapel Hill, 1959.
41 numb. l.

[NC 47]
North Carolina. Constitution.
Constitution of the state of North Carolina.
(In North Carolina. Secretary of state. North Carolina manual, 1957. Raleigh [1957] p. 39-75)

North Dakota

[ND 1]
Dakota (Ter.) Legislative Assembly.
. . . Division of Dakota Territory. Memorial of the legislative assembly of Dakota Territory, asking for the division of the present territory of Dakota, and the erection of an additional territorial organization out of the northern part of the same . . . [Washington, 1873]
2 p. ([U. S.] 42d Cong., 3d sess. House. Misc. Doc. 66)

Caption title.
January 27, 1873. Referred to the Committee on the Territories and ordered to be printed.

[ND 2]
Dakota (Ter.) Governor.
Proclamation [issued April 15, 1889, ordering an election on May 14, 1889, of delegates to the constitutional convention for the states of South Dakota and North Dakota. Bismarck, 1889]
[2] p.

Notice: "To all county clerks or auditors," 1 p., and notice: "To the clerk or auditor of . . . county," 1 p., included.

[ND 3]
Dakota (Ter.) Constitutional Convention, 1889.
Journal of the constitutional convention for North Dakota, held

[ND 3, cont.]
at Bismarck, Thursday, July 4 to August 17, 1889, together with
the enabling act of Congress and the proceedings of the Joint
Commission appointed for the equitable division of territorial
property. Bismarck, 1889.
    1 p. l., 400, 16, 32, vii p.

[ND 4]
Dakota (Ter.) Constitutional Convention, 1889.
    Official report of the proceedings and debates of the first con-
stitutional convention of North Dakota, assembled in the city of
Bismarck, July 4 to August 17, 1889. R. M. Tuttle, official
stenographer. Bismarck, 1889.
    935, lxiv p.

    Constitution of North Dakota—1889; lxiv p. at end.

[ND 5]
A Socialist Constitution for North Dakota. Do you want that or
    the constitution that has stood the test of 25 years. A care-
    ful digest and comparison . . . Bismarck [1917?]
    24 p.

[ND 6]
North Dakota. Constitution.
    The constitution of the state of North Dakota, with all amend-
ments adopted to and including November 2, 1920. Annotated.
Published under legislative authority, by Thomas Hall, secretary
of state. Edited by Maurice W. Duffy, deputy. [Fargo, 1920]
    148 p.

[ND 7]
North Dakota. Constitution.
    The constitution of the state of North Dakota, with all amend-
ments adopted to and including June 27, 1950 . . . by Thomas
Hall, secretary of state. Compiled by Charles Liessman.
[Bismarck? 1950?]
    130 p., maps.

Ohio

[Oh 1]
Ohio. Constitutional Convention, 1802.
Journal of the convention of the territory of the United States north-west of the Ohio, begun and held at Chillicothe, on Monday, the first day of November, A. D. one thousand eight hundred and two, and the independence of the United States the twenty-seventh. Chillicothe, 1802.

(In Ohio. Secretary of state. Annual report, 1875-1876. p. 35-74)

[Oh 2]
Ohio. Constitution.
Letter from Thomas Worthington, inclosing an ordinance passed by the convention of the state of Ohio, together with the constitution, formed and agreed to by the convention for the said state, and sundry propositions, submitted to the Congress of the United States. [Washington, 1802]
35 p.

Letter of transmittal from Thomas Worthington to the speaker of the House of Representatives: p. 3.

[Oh 3]
Ohio. Constitutional Convention, 1850-1851.
Report of the debates and proceedings of the convention for

[Oh 3, cont.]
the revision of the constitution of the state of Ohio, 1850-1851.
J. V. Smith, official reporter to the convention. Columbus, 1851.
2 v.

"Constitution of the State of Ohio": p. 856-866.

[Oh 4]
Ohio. Constitutional Convention, 1850-1851.
Standing rules of the constitutional convention of the state of
Ohio, adopted in convention, Thursday, May 16, 1850. Colum-
bus, 1850.
10 p.

[Oh 5]
Ohio. Secretary of State.
Reply of the secretary of state in answer to a resolution of the
Ohio constitutional convention. [May 23, 1850. n. p., 1850?]
4 p.

Cover title.

[Oh 6]
Ohio. Secretary of State.
Report of the secretary of state to the Ohio constitutional con-
vention. In accordance with resolutions passed in convention,
May 13, 1850, calling for certain information from the several
courts of common pleas of this state, the Commercial Court of
Cincinnati, and the Superior Court of Cleveland. In convention,
Friday, June 7, 1850. Columbus, 1850.
8 p.

[Oh 7]
Ohio. Constitution.
The constitution of the state of Ohio, passed in convention,
March 10, 1851; adopted by the vote of the people, June 17, took
effect, September 1, 1851. With an index. Columbus, 1852.
56 p.

[Oh 8]
Ohio. Constitution.
Constitutions of 1802 and 1851, with notes to the decisions construing them, and references to the constitutional debates. By George B. Okey and John H. Morton.

(Appended to sessions laws, sixtieth assembly, adjourned session. 1873. 151 p.)

[Oh 9]
Ohio. Constitutional Convention, 1873-1874.
Official report of the proceedings and debates of the third constitutional convention of Ohio, assembled in the city of Columbus, on Tuesday, May 13, 1873. J. G. Adel, official reporter . . . Cleveland, 1873-1874.
2 v. in 4.

V. II, pt. 1-3, have title: Official report of the proceedings and debates of the third constitutional convention of Ohio; assembled in . . . Cincinnati . . . December 2, 1873.
The convention met in Columbus, from May 13 to August 8, 1873; in Cincinnati, from December 2, 1873 to May 15, 1874.
The constitution proposed by this convention was rejected by the people.
"Constitution of the state of Ohio": v. II, pt. 3, p. 3545-3560.

[Oh 10]
Ohio. Constitution.
Constitution of the state of Ohio, agreed upon in convention May 14, 1874. Columbus, 1874.
42 p.

Cover title.
This constitution was rejected by the people.

[Oh 11]
Patterson, Isaac Franklin, comp.
The constitutions of Ohio, amendments, and proposed amend-

[Oh 11, cont.]
ments, including the Ordinance of 1787, the act of Congress dividing the Northwest Territory, and the acts of Congress creating and recognizing the state of Ohio; complete original texts, with historical data, records of the vote cast, contemporary newspaper comment, detailed comparisons, and historical introduction. Cleveland, 1912.

3 p. l., [3]-358 p. incl. 3 facsims.

[Oh 12]
Ohio. Constitutional Convention, 1912.
The Constitution of the United States and the constitution of Ohio. Constitutional conventions of Ohio and their work. Published by authority of the constitutional convention of 1912. C. B. Galbreath, secretary. Columbus, 1912.

184 p.

"Constitution of the United States—1787": p. 7-20; "The Ordinance of 1787": p. 21-26.

"Constitution of the State of Ohio of 1802": p. 32-51; "The Constitution of the State of Ohio of 1851, as amended to January 1, 1912": p. 54-126; "Constitution of the State of Ohio, adopted in Convention, May 14, 1874": p. 133-169.

"Act providing for fourth Constitutional Convention": p. 178-182.

Bibliography: p. 184.

[Oh 13]
Ohio. Constitutional Convention, 1912.
Journal of the constitutional convention of the state of Ohio; convened January 9, 1912; adjourned June 7, 1912; reconvened and adjourned without day August 26, 1912 . . . Columbus, 1912.

1203 p.

Rules: p. 930-941.

Ordinance of 1787, constitutions of Ohio, 1802, 1851, proposed constitution of 1874, and amendments proposed by the constitutional convention of 1912: p. 942-1072.

[Oh 14]
Ohio. Constitutional Convention, 1912.

Proceedings and debates of the constitutional convention of the state of Ohio; convened January 9, 1912; adjourned June 7, 1912; reconvened and adjourned without day August 26, 1912; Published in accordance with the provisions of an act of the General Assembly (102 O. L. 298) and by authority of the constitutional convention . . . Columbus, 1912-1913.

2 v. (2254 p.)

Vote on amendments submitted to the people by the convention, special election, September 3, 1912: v. 2, p. 2112-2114.

C. B. Galbreath, secretary of the convention; Clarence E. Walker, official reporter; E. S. Nichols, editor and proofreader.

Amendments to the constitution of Ohio; resolutions adopted in convention May 31, 1912, and signed June 1, 1912: v. 2, p. 2101-2110.

[Oh 15]
Ohio. Constitutional Convention, 1912.

New constitution for Ohio; an explanation of the work of Ohio's fourth constitutional convention by the president, Hon. Herbert S. Bigelow. Washington, 1912.

15 p. ([U. S.] 62d Cong., 2d sess. House. Doc. 863)

[Oh 16]
Ohio. Constitution.

The constitution of the state of Ohio and the several amendments submitted at the election held September 3, 1912, with the proclamation of the governor and the vote by counties on each amendment. Published by Chas. H. Graves, secretary of state. Columbus, 1913.

83 p. incl. tables.

[Oh 17]
Ohio. Constitution.

The constitution of the state of Ohio, annotated, as in force and

[Oh 17, cont.]
effect July 1, 1930. Compiled and issued by Clarence J. Brown,
secretary of state. Columbus, 1930.
   131 p.

[Oh 18]
Ohio. Constitution.
   Amendment to the constitution, proposed by initiative petition
to be submitted directly to the electors . . . [Columbus? 1930]
   [4] p.

   Caption title.

[Oh 19]
Ohio. Program Commission. Constitutional Convention Committee.
   Ohio's constitution in the making. [By] Lauren A. Glosser,
executive secretary. Columbus [1952]
   [2], 12 p.

   Cover title.
   Bibliography: back cover.

[Oh 20]
Ohio. Constitution.
   The constitution of the state of Ohio, annotated, 1957; and
Constitution of the United States; Ordinance of the Northwest
Territory, 1787; Declaration of Independence. [Reproduced from
Baldwin's Ohio revised code. Columbus, 1957]
   1 v. (various pagings)

   Issued by Ted W. Brown, secretary of state.

Oklahoma

[Ok 1]
Oklahoma (Ter.) Constitutional Convention, 1906-1907.
Proceedings of the constitutional convention of the proposed state of Oklahoma held at Guthrie, Oklahoma, November 20, 1906, to November 16, 1907. Muskogee [1907?]
1 p. l., [5]-486, 73 p.

Running title: Journal of the constitutional convention of Oklahoma.

[Ok 2]
Oklahoma (Ter.) Constitutional Convention, 1906-1907.
. . . A proposition for a complete constitution, including ordinances, preamble, bill of rights, form of government and schedule; recommended by the Republicans of the constitutional convention to be adopted as the ordinances and the constitution for the proposed state of Oklahoma. Introduction by Henry E. Asp. [Muskogee, 1907]
[3]-43 p.

Cover title.
At head of title: Proposition no. 438.

[Ok 3]
Oklahoma (Ter.) Constitutional Convention, 1906-1907.
Report of Committee on Revision, Compilation, Style and

[Ok 3, cont.]
Arrangement to the constitutional convention, Monday, February 25, 1907. Guthrie [1907]
54 p.

[Ok 4]
Oklahoma (Ter.) Constitutional Convention, 1906-1907.
Report of Committee on Revision, Compilation, Style and Arrangement to the constitutional convention, Wednesday, February 27, 1907. Guthrie [1907]
57 p., 1 l.

Cover title.

[Ok 5]
Oklahoma (Ter.) Constitutional Convention, 1906-1907.
Report of Committee on Revision, Compilation, Style and Arrangement to the constitutional convention. County boundaries and county seats. Guthrie [1907]
55, [1] p.

At head of title: 2
Errata slip inserted.

[Ok 6]
Oklahoma (Ter.) Constitutional Convention, 1906-1907.
Report of Committee on Revision, Compilation, Style and Arrangement to the constitutional convention, Friday, March 8, 1907. Guthrie [1907]
41 p.

At head of title: 3

[Ok 7]
Oklahoma (Ter.) Constitutional Convention, 1906-1907.
Report of Committee on Revision, Compilation, Style and Arrangement to the constitutional convention, Monday, March 11, 1907. Guthrie [1907]
47 p.

At head of title: 4

[Ok 8]
Oklahoma (Ter.) Constitutional Convention, 1906-1907.
Report of Committee on Revision, Compilation, Style and Arrangement to the constitutional convention, Wednesday, March 13, 1907. Guthrie [1907]
36 p.

At head of title: 5

[Ok 9]
Oklahoma (Ter.) Constitutional Convention, 1906-1907.
Report of Committee on Revision, Compilation, Style and Arrangement to the constitutional convention, Thursday, March 14, 1907. Guthrie [1907]
28 p.

At head of title: 6

[Ok 10]
Oklahoma (Ter.) Constitutional Convention, 1906-1907.
Report of the Hon. William H. Murray, president of the constitutional convention, submitted to the Senate and House of Representatives of the first legislature of Oklahoma, March 2, 1908, and ordered printed as an appendix to the journal of the House of Representatives. [Guthrie? 1908]
16 p.

[Ok 11]
Oklahoma (Ter.) Constitutional Convention, 1906-1907.
Proposed constitution of the state of Oklahoma. Printed from a copy certified by William H. Murray, president of the constitutional convention. Washington, 1907.
96 p.

"Done in open convention at the city of Guthrie in the Territory of Oklahoma on this the nineteenth day of April in the year of Our Lord one thousand nine hundred and seven. . . ."

[Ok 12]
Oklahoma. Constitution.

Constitution and enabling act of the state of Oklahoma, annotated and indexed, comprising the enabling act of the state of Oklahoma, approved June 16, 1906, amendments to the enabling act, approved March 4, 1907, and the constitution and ordinances of the state of Oklahoma, adopted by the constitutional convention, ratified by the people and approved by the President of the United States. Compiled by Clinton O. Bunn . . . and Wm. C. Bunn . . . Ardmore [1907]

195 p.

[Ok 13]
Oklahoma. Constitution.

The constitution of Oklahoma, with copious notes referring to and digesting decisions construing and applying identical and similar provisions of the constitutions and statutes of other states and of the United States, by Henry G. Snyder . . . Kansas City, Mo., 1908.

2 p. l., 3-iv, 521 p.

[Ok 14]
Oklahoma. Constitution.

The constitution and enabling act of the state of Oklahoma, annotated with references to the constitution, statutes, and decision [sic] of other states and the United States, by R. L. Williams . . . Kansas City, Mo., 1912.

3 p. l., 318 p.

[Ok 15]
Oklahoma. Constitution.

The constitution of Oklahoma and enabling act, annotated, with references to the constitution, statutes, and decisions, by Robert L. Williams . . . 2d ed., revised and annotated, containing Magna Carta, the English bill of rights, and the Constitution of the United States, with a group of federal court decisions on "New Deal" legislation. Compiled by C. W. King . . . [Guthrie, 1941]

3 p. l., 462 p., port.

[Ok 16]
——. Supplement . . . containing newly adopted amendments to the Oklahoma constitution and additional citations of court decisions. [Guthrie] 1941.
    8 p.

[Ok 17]
Oklahoma. Constitutional Survey Committee.
    Oklahoma constitutional studies of the Oklahoma Constitutional Survey and Citizen Advisory committees. Directed by H. V. Thornton. Initiated by the Oklahoma State Legislative Council. [Oklahoma City, 1947-1950]
    xxxiv, 2 l., 609 p.

    Contents:—1. What a constitution should contain, by H. V. Thornton.—2. Bill of Rights, by H. V. Thornton.—3. Amendment and revision of the constitution of Oklahoma, by J. W. Strain.—4. Legislative organization, by H. V. Thornton.—5. Bicameralism-unicameralism, by H. V. Thornton.—6. Apportionment in Oklahoma, by H. V. Thornton.—7. Direct legislation, by J. Gillespie.—8. Organization of the executive department, by H. V. Thornton.—9. The chief executive, by J. W. Strain.—10. Budget administration in Oklahoma, by H. V. Thornton.—11. The merit system among the states, by W. V. Holloway.—12. Executive and administrative agencies, by the Department of Government, University of Oklahoma.—13. Institutions and institutional control, by W. Ingler.—14. Judicial personnel, by D. L. Bowen.—15. Judicial organization and management, by D. L. Bowen.—16. Improvement of the administration of justice, by the Oklahoma Bar Association's Committee on the Improvement of the Administration of Justice.—17. County government-an analysis, by J. P. Duncan.—18. County government-forms, by J. P. Duncan.—19. County government-constitutional data, by J. P. Duncan.—20. The constitutional structure and functioning of city government in Oklahoma-an anlaysis, by J. P. Duncan.—21. City government-constitutional data, by J. P. Duncan.—22. Federal-state relations and Oklahoma's constitution, by E. Foster Dowell.

[Ok 18]
Oklahoma. Constitution.
Constitution of the state of Oklahoma, as amended to January 1, 1957. St. Paul, 1957.
75 p.

Oregon

[Or 3, cont.]
gether with the standing committees &c. [Salem, 1857]
   8 p.

[Or 4]
Oregon. Secretary of State.
   Official Republican voters' pamphlet containing proposed constitutional amendments and measures (with arguments) to be
submitted to the voters of Oregon . . . and statements of candi-
dates for nomination for state and district offices. [Salem, 1934?]
   48 p., ports.

   Cover title.

[Or 5]
Oregon. Governor's and Legislative Constitutional Committee.
   Report submitted to the governor and the forty-eighth legislative assembly. [Salem?] 1955.
   47 p.

[Or 6]
Oregon. Constitution.
   Constitution of Oregon. Salem [1960]

   (Reprinted from Oregon revised statutes, 1960. p. 999-1048)

Pennsylvania

[Pa 1]
Pennsylvania. Constitutional Convention, 1776.
   The proceedings relative to calling the conventions of 1776 and 1790. The minutes of the convention that formed the present constitution of Pennsylvania, together with the charter to William Penn, the constitutions of 1776 and 1790, and a view of the proceedings of the convention of 1776 and the Council of Censors. Harrisburg, 1825.
   v, [9]-384, iv p.

   A conference of extralegal committees of correspondence called a convention to meet at Philadelphia, July 1, to September 28, 1776, and frame a constitution. In 1789 the General Assembly called another constitutional convention, which met at Philadelphia November 24, 1789, to February 26, 1790, and rewrote the constitution. This new constitution was published for examination by the people, after which the convention reassembled on August 9 and proclaimed it September 2.

[Pa 2]
Pennsylvania. General Assembly. Senate.
   Resolutions on the subject of calling a convention, to alter and amend certain parts of the constitution of this commonwealth. In Senate, January 9, 1812. [n. p., n. d.]
   7 p.

[Pa 3]
Pennsylvania. General Assembly. Senate. Select Committee to
Whom Were Referred the Petitions of Citizens Praying for
the Passage of a Law Authorizing the Call of a Convention
to Alter the Constitution.
Report . . . Read in the Senate, February 20, 1833. Harrisburg,
1833.
7 p.

[Pa 4]
Pennsylvania. Constitutional Convention, 1837-1838.
Journal of the convention of the state of Pennsylvania, to pro-
pose amendments to the constitution, commenced and held at the
State Capitol in Harrisburg, on the second day of May, 1837.
Harrisburg, and Philadelphia, 1837-1838.
2 v., folded chart.
V. 2: Minutes of the Committee of the Whole.

[Pa 5]
Pennsylvania. Constitutional Convention, 1837-1838.
Proceedings and debates of the convention of the commonwealth of Pennsylvania, to propose amendments to the constitution, commenced and held at Harrisburg, on the second day of
May, 1837. Reported by John Agg, stenographer to the convention; assisted by Messrs. Kingman, Drake, and M'Kinley . . .
Harrisburg, 1837-1839.
14 v.

[Pa 6]
Pennsylvania. Constitutional Convention, 1837-1838.
Convention directory: containing the rules and orders of the
convention, which assembled at Harrisburg, Penn., May 2, 1837;
with the names of the delegates, places of abode, and nearest
post-office . . . Harrisburg, 1837.
42 p.

[Pa 7]
An appeal to the people of the commonwealth of Pennsylvania, in
    behalf of the constitution. Read, reflect, and decide. [n. p.]
    1838.
    29 p.

[Pa 8]
Pennsylvania. Constitution.
Constitution of Pennsylvania, 1838.

(In Thorpe, Francis Newton, comp. The federal and state constitutions, colonial charters, and other organic laws of the states,
territories, and colonies now or heretofore forming the United
States of America. Washington, 1909. v. 5, p. 3104-3117)

[Pa 9]
Pennsylvania. Constitution.
Amendments to the constitution of 1838. [Ratified 1850, 1857,
1864, and 1872]

(In Thorpe, Francis Newton, comp. The federal and state constitutions, colonial charters, and other organic laws of the states,
territories, and colonies now or heretofore forming the United
States of America. Washington, 1909. v. 5, p. 3117-3120)

[Pa 10]
Pennsylvania. Constitutional Convention, 1872-1873.
Journal of the convention to amend the constitution of Penn-
sylvania: convened at Harrisburg, November 12, 1872; adjourned
November 27, to meet at Philadelphia, January 7, 1873 . . .
Harrisburg, 1873.
    2 v. (1424 p.)

[Pa 11]
Pennsylvania. Constitutional Convention, 1872-1873.
Debates of the convention to amend the constitution of Penn-
sylvania: convened at Harrisburg, November 12, 1872; ad-
journed, November 27, to meet at Philadelphia, January 7, 1873
. . . Harrisburg, 1873.
    9 v.

[Pa 12]
Pennsylvania. Secretary of the Commonwealth.

Statistical and other information for the constitutional convention of Pennsylvania. Prepared by Francis Jordan, secretary of the commonwealth; in compliance with the act of assembly authorizing said convention. Harrisburg, 1872.

54 p.

[Pa 13]
Pennsylvania. Constitutional Convention, 1872-1873.

Proceedings of the trial of Hon. James Boyd, of Montgomery Col, Pa., June 14, 1873, by his colleagues of the constitutional convention. Philadelphia, 1874.

75 p.

[Pa 14]
Pennsylvania. Constitutional Convention, 1872-1873.

. . . [Report] to the people of Pennsylvania. [Philadelphia, 1873?]

8 p.

[Pa 15]
An answer to the report of Constitutional Commission, as made to the legislature of Pennsylvania, at the session of 1875; by members of late constitutional convention from Luzerne County. Philadelphia, 1875.

20 p.

[Pa 16]
Pennsylvania. Constitution.

New constitution. Printed by order of the convention. To be submitted to a vote of the people, Tuesday, December 16, 1873. [Philadelphia, 1873]

48 p.

[Pa 17]
Pennsylvania. Constitution.
The constitution of the commonwealth of Pennsylvania. With an introduction, notes and references, and an exhaustive index: showing . . . the changes made by the constitution of 1873-1874. By H. E. Wallace and D. Sanders. Philadelphia, 1874.
64 p.

[Pa 18]
Pennsylvania. Constitution.
An examination of the constitution of Pennsylvania. Exhibiting the derivation and history of its several provisions, with observations and occasional notes thereon, references to judicial and other opinions upon their construction and application, to statutes for their enforcement, and to parallel provisions in the constitutions of other American states. By Charles R. Buckalew. Philadelphia, 1883.
xi, 349 p.

[Pa 19]
Pennsylvania. Constitution.
Constitution of Pennsylvania analytically indexed and with index of prohibited legislation. By James McKirdy, assistant director. Harrisburg, 1912.
118 p. (Legislative Reference Bureau. [Bulletin, no. 1])
Amended November 5, 1901, and November 2, 1909.

[Pa 20]
Pennsylvania. Commission on Constitutional Amendment and Revision.
Journal of proceedings . . . [and appendix]. Harrisburg, 1920. 3 v., folded chart.
Compiled by Francis Newton Thorpe, commissioner from Allegheny County.
V. 2 includes also reports from committees, memoranda and briefs, constitution of 1873, tentative draft of constitution, indexes.

[Pa 21]
Pennsylvania. Commission on Constitutional Amendment and
    Revision.
Report of the commission to the General Assembly. December
15, 1920. [Harrisburg? 1921?]
    414 p.

[Pa 23]
Pennsylvania. Constitution.
Constitution of the commonwealth of Pennsylvania.

(In Pennsylvania. Pennsylvania state manual, formerly Smull's
Legislative Handbook, 1957-1958. Harrisburg, 1959. p. 33-73)

[Pa 24]
Pennsylvania. Commission on Constitutional Revision.
Report. [Harrisburg] 1959.
    226 p.

Rhode Island

[RI 1]
Rhode Island (Colony) Charters.
Charter of Rhode Island and Providence Plantations—1663.

(In Thorpe, Francis Newton, comp. The federal and state constitutions, colonial charters, and other organic laws of the states, territories, and colonies now or heretofore forming the United States of America. Washington, 1909. v. 6, p. 3211-3222)

[RI 2]
Rhode Island. Constitution.
Constitution of the state of Rhode-Island and Providence Plantations, as adopted by the convention, assembled at Newport, June 21, 1824. Providence, 1824.
18 p.

The constitution was rejected.

[RI 3]
Rhode Island. Constitutional Convention, 1834.
An address to the people of Rhode-Island, from the convention assembled at Providence, on the 22d day of February, and again on the 12th day of March, 1834, to promote the establishment of a state constitution. Providence, 1834.
60 p.

The convention did not complete a constitution.

[RI 4]
U. S. Congress. House. Select Committee on Rhode Island.
Rhode Island memorial . . . Minority . . . report . . . [Washington, 1845]
172 p. ([U. S.] 28th Cong., 1st sess. House Rept. 81)

Submitted by Mr. Causin. June 17, 1844, read and laid upon the table. January 2, 1834, ordered that 5,000 copies be printed.

Relates to troubles in Rhode Island over adoption of a state constitution. Includes the text of the so-called People's Constitution, adopted November 18, 1841, by a convention which was called by a committee appointed at a mass meeting of the people held in Providence on May 5, 1841; also the text of the so-called Landholders' Constitution, the product of a convention authorized by the General Assembly to meet at Providence from November 1, 1841, to February 19, 1842.

[RI 5]
Rhode Island. General Assembly. Committee on Action of General Assembly on Constitution.
Report of the Committee on the Action of the General Assembly on the subject of the constitution. [Providence, 1842]
15 p.

Relates to the rejection of the so-called Landholders' Constitution and the adoption of the so-called People's Constitution.

"An act in relation to offences against the sovereign power of the State": p. 13-15.

[RI 6]
Rhode Island. Constitutional Convention, 1842.
Journal of the convention assembled to frame a constitution for the state of Rhode Island, at Newport, September 12, 1842. Providence, 1859.
69 p.

[RI 7]
Rhode Island. Constitution.
The constitution of the state of Rhode-Island and Providence Plantations, as adopted by the convention, assembled at Newport, September, 1842. Providence, 1842.
24 p.

[RI 8]
Duff, Henry J.
Petition of Henry J. Duff, and others, for an alteration of the state constitution. To the Honorable General Assembly of the state of Rhode Island, at their May session, A. D. 1846. [Providence, 1846]
[4] p.

Caption title.

[RI 9]
Rhode Island. General Assembly. House of Representatives. Committee on the Petition of Henry J. Duff.
Report of the Committee on the Petition of Henry J. Duff, and others, by Sylvester G. Sherman, Esq., chairman, . . . made to the House of Representatives of the legislature of Rhode Island, at the January session, 1847. [Providence? 1847?]
16 p.

Caption title.

[RI 10]
Rhode Island. Constitution.
Articles of amendment [to the constitution of 1842, ratified 1854 and 1864]

(In Thorpe, Francis Newton, comp. The federal and state constitutions, colonial charters, and other organic laws of the states, territories, and colonies now or heretofore forming the United States of America. Washington, 1909. v. 6, p. 3235-3236)

[RI 11]
Rhode Island. General Assembly. Joint Select Committee on
    Changes in the Constitution.
    Report of Joint Select Committee on Changes in the Constitu-
tion, made to the General Assembly, at its January session, A. D.
1882. Providence, 1882.
    21, [1] p.

    Signed by the committee, W. P. Sheffield and five others.

[RI 12]
Rhode Island. Supreme Court.
    Opinion of the Court on the power of the General Assembly to
call a constitutional convention, made to the Senate at its January
session, 1883. Providence, 1883.
    7 p.

[RI 13]
Rhode Island. Constitution.
    Articles of amendment [to the constitution of 1842, ratified
1886, 1888, 1889, 1892, and 1893]

    (In Thorpe, Francis Newton, comp. The federal and state con-
stitutions, colonial charters, and other organic laws of the states,
territories, and colonies now or heretofore forming the United
States of America. Washington, 1909. v. 6, p. 3236-3237)

[RI 14]
Rhode Island. Commission to Revise the Constitution.
    Report of the Commission to Revise the Constitution made to
the General Assembly at its January session, 1898. Providence,
1898.
    47 p.

    Revised constitution: p. [15]-47.

[RI 15]
Rhode Island. Constitution.
    Articles of amendment [to the constitution of 1842, ratified
1900 and 1903]

[RI 15, cont.]
(In Thorpe, Francis Newton, comp. The federal and state constitutions, colonial charters, and other organic laws of the states, territories, and colonies now or heretofore forming the United States of America. Washington, 1909. v. 6, p. 3237-3240)

[RI 17]
Rhode Island. Supreme Court.
[Opinion of the Supreme Court, given to the Senate of Rhode Island, February 4, 1909. Providence, 1909]
    p. [611]-621

"Opinion . . . upon the division for submission separately to the electors of certain amendments to the Constitution of the State proposed in a resolution passed at the January session, A. D. 1908, of the General Assembly."–p. [3]
    Signed by Edward C. Dubois, J. T. Blodgett, C. H. Johnson, C. F. Parkhurst, and W. H. Sweetland.

[RI 18]
Rhode Island. Commission to Draft and Report an Act Providing for a House of Representatives.
    Report of Commission to Draft and Report an Act Providing for a House of Representatives made to His Excellency Aram J. Pothier, governor of Rhode Island. August 1, 1910. Providence, 1910.
    25, 84 p., maps.

Includes an act dividing the cities and certain towns of the state into representative districts and carrying into effect article XIII of amendments to the constitution.

[RI 19]
Rhode Island. Commission to Consider the Amendment and Revision of the Constitution.
    Report of Commission to Consider the Amendment and Revision of the Constitution, presented to the General Assembly at its January session, 1915. Providence, 1915.
    17, 47 p.

[RI 19, cont.]
Includes the constitution as amended, women's suffrage amendment, and minority report.

[RI 20]
Rhode Island. Supreme Court.
Advisory opinion of the Supreme Court of Rhode Island upon questions relating to a constitutional convention. April 1, 1935. Affirmative and negative briefs submitted. [Providence, 1935]
462 p.

[RI 21]
Rhode Island. Constitution.
Constitution of the state of Rhode Island and Providence Plantations with the amendments thereto. Providence, 1942.
44 p.

[RI 22]
Rhode Island. Constitutional Convention, 1944.
Proceedings of the limited constitutional convention of the state of Rhode Island, held on the twenty-eighth day of March, A. D. 1944 . . . [Providence, 1944]
37 p.

[RI 23]
Rhode Island. Constitution.
Amendments to the constitution of the state of Rhode Island and Providence Plantations since 1944. 1951 supplement. Providence, 1951.
16 p.

[RI 24]
Rhode Island. Constitutional Convention, 1951.
Proceedings of the limited constitutional convention of the state of Rhode Island, held on the 1st, 2d, and 3d days of June, A. D. 1951, as provided for under Chapter 2705 of the public laws of Rhode Island, 1951. [Providence] 1951.
194 p.

[RI 25]
Rhode Island. Constitution.
   Constitution of the state of Rhode Island and Providence Plantations.

   (In Rhode Island. Dept. of state. Manual, with rules and orders, for the use of the General Assembly of the state of Rhode Island, 1959-1960. Providence, 1959. p. 39-99)

South Carolina

[SC 1]
South Carolina (Colony) Provincial Congress.
Journal of the Provincial Congress of South Carolina, 1776.
Charles-Town: printed; London: reprinted, 1776.
133 p.

[SC 2]
South Carolina. Constitution.
Constitution of South Carolina—1776. [n. p., n. d.]
p. [1615]-1620.
Caption title.

[SC 3]
South Carolina. General Assembly.
A bill for establishing the constitution of the state of South
Carolina. Charles-Town, 1777.
23 p.

[SC 4]
South Carolina. Constitution.
Constitution of South Carolina—1778.
(In Thorpe, Francis Newton, comp. The federal and state con-
stitutions, colonial charters, and other organic laws of the states,
territories, and colonies now or heretofore forming the United
States of America. Washington, 1909. v. 6, p. 3248-3257)
Framed by the General Assembly and passed as an "act":
March 19, 1778. Went into effect in November.

[SC 5]
South Carolina. Constitutional Convention, 1790.
Journal. May 10, 1790-June 3, 1790, edited by Francis M. Hutson. Columbia, 1946.
38 p.

[SC 6]
South Carolina. Constitution.
Constitution of South Carolina—1790.

(In Thorpe, Francis Newton, comp. The federal and state constitutions, colonial charters, and other organic laws of the states, territories, and colonies now or heretofore forming the United States of America. Washington, 1909. v. 6, p. 3258-3265)

[SC 7]
South Carolina. Constitution.
Amendments to the constitution of 1790 [ratified 1808, 1810, 1816, 1820, 1828, 1834, and 1856]

(In Thorpe, Francis Newton, comp. The federal and state constitutions, colonial charters, and other organic laws of the states, territories, and colonies now or heretofore forming the United States of America. Washington, 1909. v. 6, p. 3265-3269

[SC 8]
South Carolina. Convention, 1860-1862.
Journal of the convention of the people of South Carolina, held in 1860, 1861, and 1862, together with the ordinances, reports, resolutions, etc. Columbia, 1862.
873 p.

"The Constitution of the State of South Carolina, April 8, 1864."

[SC 9]
South Carolina. Constitutional Convention, 1865.
Journal of the convention of the people of South Carolina, held in Columbia, S. C., September, 1865. Together with the

[SC 9, cont.]
ordinances, reports, resolutions, etc. Columbia, 1865.
216 p.

"Constitution of the State of South Carolina": p. [137]-178.

[SC 10]
South Carolina. Constitutional Convention, 1868.
Proceedings of the constitutional convention of South Carolina, held at Charleston, S. C., beginning January 14, and ending March 17, 1868. Including the debates and proceedings. Reported by J. Woodruff, phonographic reporter. Charleston, 1868.
2 v. in 1. (iv, 926 p.)

[SC 11]
South Carolina. Constitution.
The constitution of the state of South Carolina, with the ordinances thereunto appended, adopted by the constitutional convention, which was held at Charleston, and adjourned on the 17th [of] March, 1868. Charleston, 1868.
46 p.

[SC 12]
South Carolina. Constitution.
Amendments [to the constitution of 1868, ratified 1873, 1875, 1878, and 1880]

(In Thorpe, Francis Newton, comp. The federal and state constitutions, colonial charters, and other organic laws of the states, territories, and colonies now or heretofore forming the United States of America. Washington, 1909. v. 6, p. 3305-3306)

[SC 13]
South Carolina. Constitutional Convention, 1895.
Journal of the constitutional convention of the state of South Carolina. Begun to be holden at Columbia, S. C., on Tuesday, the tenth day of September, anno Domini eighteen hundred and ninety-five, and continued with divers adjournments until Wed-

[SC 13, cont.]
nesday, the fourth day of December, anno Domini eighteen hundred and ninety-five, when finally adjourned . . . Columbia, 1895.
   741, 64 p.

[SC 14]
South Carolina. Constitution.
   Constitution of the state of South Carolina, ratified in convention, December 4, 1895. Columbia, 1895.
   109 p.

[SC 15]
U. S. Constitution.
   Constitution of United States of America and amendments and of the state of South Carolina as amended, April 2, 1954.
[Columbia, 1954?]
   150 p.

South Dakota

[SD 1]
Dakota (Ter.) Constitutional Convention, 1883.
Journal of the constitutional convention of that part of Dakota south of the forty-sixth parallel of latitude . . . 1883.

(In South Dakota. State historical collections. South Dakota historical collections . . . 1942. v. 21, p. [291]-467)

[SD 2]
Dakota (Ter.) Constitutional Convention, 1883.
A memorial to the President and the Congress of the United States setting forth the especial reasons and facts upon which the people of Dakota base their action and their claim to admission. [n. p., 1883?]
1 p. l., 16 p.

[SD 3]
Dakota (Ter.) Constitutional Convention, 1885.
Journal of the proceedings of the constitutional convention held under an act of the legislature at Sioux Falls, Dakota, September, 1885. A. J. Edgerton, president. John Cain, secretary. [Sioux Falls, 1885]
1 p. l., 77 p. incl. form.

The constitution adopted by the convention . . .: p. 60-74

[SD 4]
Dakota (Ter.) Constitutional Convention, 1885.
[Constitutional debates. South Dakota, 1885, 1889] Huron, 1907-[n. d.]
2 v.

Published under the editorial supervision of Doane Robinson, state librarian.
Debates of the constitutional convention of 1885 which formulated the constitution . . . and constitutional convention of 1889 which revised the same. The convention of 1885 sat from September 8-25, 1885; that of 1889 from July 4-August 5, 1889.
"The debates of the Convention of 1883 were not preserved.:- v. 2, p. [1]
Contents:—v. 1. Dakota constitutional convention held at Sioux Falls, September, 1885.—v. 2. South Dakota constitutional convention, held at Sioux Falls, July, 1889.

[SD 5]
Dakota (Ter.) Constitutional Convention, 1885.
Presentation of Dakota's claims, and memorial praying for admission. The constitution adopted by the convention held at Sioux Falls, Dakota, September, 1885. Sioux Falls [1885?]
[2], 62 p.

Cover title: Dakota. Claims for admission. The constitution.
As South Dakota was not admitted as a state until 1889, another convention met on July 4 of that year and readopted the constitution of 1885, with minor changes.

[SD 6]
Dakota (Ter.) Constitutional Convention, 1889.
Journal of the constitutional convention of South Dakota, July, 1889. Sioux Falls, 1889.
226, iii p.

Constitution: p. 162-223.

[SD 7]
South Dakota. Constitution.

Constitution, 1929. State of South Dakota. Annotated. Annotations to May 1, 1927, by Honorable John Howard Gates, judge of the Supreme Court . . . Annotations covering decisions printed May 1, 1927, to March 15, 1929, by Honorable Dwight Campbell, judge of the Supreme Court . . . Published by Gladys Pyle, secretary of state . . . [Pierre? 1929?]

143 p.

[SD 8]
South Dakota. Constitution.

Constitution of the state of South Dakota. Pierre, 1957.

46 p.

Cover title.

Tennessee

[Tn 1]
Tennessee. Constitutional Convention, 1796.
Journal of the proceedings of a convention, began and held at Knoxville, on the eleventh day of January, one thousand seven hundred and ninety-six, for the purpose of forming a constitution, or form of government, for the permanent government of the people. [Knoxville, 1796. Reprinted: Nashville, 1852]
32 p.

[Tn 2]
Tennessee. Constitution.
Constitution of the state of Tennessee. Unanimously established in convention at Knoxville, on the sixth day of February, one thousand seven hundred and ninety-six. Philadelphia, 1796.
[5]-33 p.

[Tn 3]
Tennessee. Constitutional Convention, 1834.
Journal of the convention of the state of Tennessee. Convened for the purpose of revising and amending the constitution thereof. Held in Nashville . . . Nashville, 1834.
415 p.

[Tn 4]
Tennessee. Constitution.
Constitution of the state of Tennessee as revised and amended
by the people of said state by their delegates assembled in convention, begun and holden at Nashville on the 3d Monday of May
1834. Nashville, 1834.

[Tn 5]
Tennessee. Constitutional Convention, 1861.
Proceedings of the E. T. Convention held at Knoxville, May 30
and 31, 1861, and at Greenville, on the 17th day of June, 1861,
and the following days. Knoxville, 1861.
28 p.

"Although secession had been voted down early in 1861, a
second referendum approved withdrawal from the Union. Tennessee was bitterly divided in loyalty; it was the last of the eleven
states to join the Confederacy. Until 1862 East Tennessee continued to be represented in the U. S. Congress by Andrew Johnson,
who established a loyal government in the State."—The Oxford
companion to American history. New York, 1866. p. 779.

[Tn 7]
Tennessee. Constitutional Convention, 1870.
Journal of the proceedings of the convention of delegates
elected by the people of Tennessee, to amend, revise, or form and
make a new constitution, for the state. Assembled in the city of
Nashville, January 10, 1870. Nashville, 1870.
467 p.

"The Constitution of the State of Tennessee adopted . . . February 23, 1870": p. [411]-440.

[Tn 8]
Tennessee. Constitution.
The constitution of the state of Tennessee, fully annotated,
with indexed notes drawn from the decisions of the Supreme
Court of Tennessee; and also from the decisions of the Supreme

[Tn 8, cont.]
Court of the United States, construing each particular constitutional provision, and bearing upon kindred subjects . . . Annotated and edited by Robert T. Shannon. Nashville, 1915.
5-863 p.

Declaration of Independence, Articles of Confederation and Perpetual Union, and the Constitution of the United States: p. 8-67.
"Schedule to amendments of 1853": p. 626-627.
"Constitutional amendments of 1865": p. 627.
"Schedule to the amendments of 1865": p. 628-635.

[Tn 9]
Tennessee. Constitution Revision Commission.
Report. [Nashville, 1946]
61 p.

Cover title.

[Tn 10]
Tennessee. Limited Constitutional Convention, 1953.
The journal and debates of the constitutional convention. Held at the State Capitol, Nashville, Tennessee. [Nashville, 1954]
vi, 1235 p.

Cover title: Journal and proceedings, constitutional convention, state of Tennessee, 1953.

[Tn 11]
Tennessee. Constitution.
Constitution of the state of Tennessee. [Nashville, 1956]
48 p. ports., facsim.

Includes "A brief historical sketch of Tennessee" and "Excerpts from an address by Dr. Robert H. White, State historian, to the Constitutional Convention of 1953 at Nashville, May 13, 1953."

[Tn 12]
Tennessee. Constitutional Convention, 1959.

The journal and debates of the constitutional convention, held‘ at the State Capitol, Nashville, Tennessee. [Nashville, 1959]
   vi, 416 p.

Cover title: Journal and transcript of the proceedings of the constitutional convention, state of Tennessee, 1959.

[Tn 13]
Tennessee. Constitution.

The constitution of the state of Tennessee. [Nashville, 1961]
   60 p. ports., facsims.

Includes "A brief historical sketch of Tennessee" and "Excerpts from an address by Dr. Robert H. White, State historian, to the Constitutional Convention of 1953 at Nashville, May 13, 1953."

Texas

[Tx 1]
Texas. Constitutional Convention, 1845.
Journals of the convention assembled at the city of Austin on the fourth of July, 1845, for the purpose of framing a constitution for the state of Texas. Austin, 1845.
378 p.

[Tx 2]
Texas. Constitutional Convention, 1845.
Debates of the Texas convention. By Wm. F. Weeks, reporter. Published by authority of the convention. Houston, 1846.
759 p.

[Tx 3]
Texas. Constitutional Convention, 1845.
Standing rules for the government of the convention of Texas, assembled at Austin, July 4, 1845. [Austin, 1845]
7 p.

[Tx 4]
Texas. Constitutional Convention, 1845.
Report of the Committee on the Bill of Rights and General Provisions of the Constitution. [Austin, 1845]
4 p.

[Tx 5]

Texas. Constitutional Convention, 1845.

Report of the Committee on the Executive Department, of the Constitution and Militia. July 11, 1845. [Austin, 1845]

8 p.

[Tx 6]

Texas. Constitutional Convention, 1845.

Report of the Committee on the Judiciary Department, July 12, 1845. [Austin, 1845]

[2] p.

[Tx 7]

Texas. Constitution.

Constitution of the state of Texas (adopted unanimously in convention, at the city of Austin, 1845). An ordinance in relation to colonization contracts. An ordinance assenting to the proposals of the United States Congress for the annexation of Texas. Houston, 1845.

32 p.

[Tx 8]

Texas. Convention, 1861.

Journal of the Secession Convention of Texas, 1861. Edited from the original in the Department of State by Ernest William Winkler, state librarian. [Austin] 1912.

469, [1] p., fold. facsim.

At head of title: Texas Library and Historical Commission. The State Library.

Appendixes: Address to the people of Texas.—Reports of the Committee on Public Safety.—List of the delegates.—Certificates of election.

[Tx 9]

Texas. Constitution.

The constitution of the state of Texas, as amended in 1861. The Constitution of the Confederate States of America. The ordi-

[Tx 9, cont.]
nances of the Texas convention, and an address to the people of
Texas. Printed by order of the convention and the Senate.
Austin, 1861.
  40, 40 p.

[Tx 10]
Texas. Constitutional Convention, 1866.
  Journal of the Texas state convention, assembled at Austin,
February 7, 1866. Adjourned April 2, 1866. Austin, 1866.
  391 p.

[Tx 11]
Texas. Governor, 1865-1866 (A. J. Hamilton)
  Message of Governor A. J. Hamilton to the Texas state convention. Delivered February 10, 1866. Austin, 1866.
  14 p.

  Relates to the framing of a new constitution and the reconstruction of Texas after the Civil War.

[Tx 12]
Texas. Constitutional Convention, 1866.
  The minority report, in favor of extending the right of suffrage, with certain limitations, to all men without distinction of
race or color. Made in the Texas Reconstruction Convention, by
E. Degener. February 24, 1866. Austin, 1866.
  16 p.

[Tx 13]
Texas. Constitution.
  The constitution, as amended, and ordinances of the convention of 1866, together with the proclamation of the governor de-
claring the ratification of the amendments to the constitution, and
the general laws of the regular session of the eleventh legislature of
the state of Texas. By authority. Austin, 1866 [reprinted 1898]
  31, [1] p.

  Reprinted from The laws of Texas, 1822-1897. Compiled and
arranged by H. P. N. Gammel. Austin, 1898. v. 5, p. [855]-886.

[Tx 14]
Texas. Constitutional Convention, 1868-1869.
    Journal of the Reconstruction Convention, which met at Austin, Texas . . . Austin, 1870.
        2 v. (1089, 576 p.)

[Tx 15]
Texas. Constitutional Convention, 1868-1869.
    Ordinances passed by the constitutional convention, at Austin, Texas, June 1, 1868. Austin, 1870.
        143 p.

[Tx 16]
Texas. Constitutional Convention, 1868-1869.
    Report of Special Committee on Lawlessness and Violence in Texas. Austin, 1868.
        14 p.

[Tx 17]
Texas. Constitutional Convention, 1868-1869.
    Constitution of the state of West Texas. [Austin? 1869?]
        35, [1] p.

    "Prepared by authorization of the resolution of the Texas Constitutional Convention of 1868-1869 appointing commissioners to present to the federal Congress a request for the division of Texas into two or more states."—New York Public Library Bulletin, February 1937. p. 98.

[Tx 18]
Texas. Constitution.
    Constitution of the state of Texas. Letter from General Reynolds, transmitting a copy of the constitution of the state of Texas, ratified at the election held November 30 and December 1, 2, and 3, 1869. [Washington? 1870]
        27 p. ([U. S.] 41st Cong., 2d sess. House. Misc. Doc. 82)

    Caption title.

[Tx 19]
Texas. Constitutional Convention, 1875.
Journal of the constitutional convention of the state of Texas, begun and held at the city of Austin, September 6, 1875. Galveston, 1875.
821, xviii p.

[Tx 20]
Texas. Constitutional Convention, 1875.
Debates in the Texas constitutional convention of 1875, edited by Seth Shepard McKay . . . Austin [c1930]
3 p. l., 471 p.

[Tx 21]
Texas. Constitutional Convention, 1875.
Address to the people of Texas. [By a committee of members of the convention appointed to explain the new constitution and ordinances adopted by the convention. Austin? 1875?]
8 p. (Tracts on American constitutional law and history)

[Tx 22]
Texas. Constitution.
Constitution of the state of Texas, adopted by the constitutional convention, begun and held at the city of Austin, on the sixth day of September, 1875. Official. Galveston [1875?]
36 p.

Cover title.

[Tx 23]
Texas. Constitution.
Constitution of the state of Texas, adopted by the constitutional convention convened at Austin, September 6, 1875; ratified by the people; declared adopted by proclamation of the governor, March 4, 1876, and effective April 18, 1876; with annotations of the decisions of this state to date, 1922. And the Constitution of the United States and amendments thereto,

[Tx 23, cont.]
with many annotations thereunder, Magna Carta, Declaration of
Independence of United States, Articles of Confederation and
Perpetual Union between the States, admission of states into the
Union, formation of territories, electoral votes for president and
vice president, justices of the Supreme Court of United States and
cabinet officers. Annotated by J. W. Moffett . . . Austin, 1922.
     3 p. l., 533 p. incl. tables.

[Tx 24]
Texas. Constitution.
     Vernon's annotated constitution of the state of Texas. Special
feature: interpretive commentaries by A. J. Thomas, Jr., and Ann
Van Wynen Thomas. Kansas City, Mo. [1955]

[Tx 25]
Texas. Constitution.
     Fundamentals of the Texas constitution, including in the ap-
pendix the proposed amendments to be voted on in November,
1957 and 1958. By Alvan Penn Cagle. Waco, 1957.
     266 p.

[Tx 26]
Citizens Advisory Committee on Revision of the Constitution
     of the State of Texas.
     Interim report to the fifty-sixth legislature and the people of
Texas . . . March 1, 1959 [Austin? 1959]
     [1], v. numb. l., 57 p.

Utah

[Ut 1]
Utah (Ter.) Constitutional Convention, 1860.
. . . Utah Territory. Memorial of a convention of the people of the territory of Utah, accompanied by a state constitution, asking admission into the Union. [Washington, 1860]
11 p. ([U. S.] 36th Cong., 2d sess. House. Misc. Doc. 10)

Caption title.
"December 31, 1860. Referred to the Committee on the Territories and ordered to be printed."

[Ut 2]
Utah (Ter.) Constitutional Convention, 1872.
. . . Admission of Utah into the Union. Memorial of the convention to frame a constitution for the admission of Utah into the Union as a state, convened at Salt Lake City, February 19, 1872; with the constitution of the state of Deseret, adopted in convention March 2, 1872, ratified by vote of the people, March 18, 1872. [Washington, 1872]
21 p. ([U. S.] 42d Cong., 2d sess. House. Misc. Doc. 165)

Caption title.
Admission to statehood, under this constitution, refused by Congress.

[Ut 3]
Utah (Ter.) Constitutional Convention, 1882.
Constitution of the state of Utah. Adopted by the convention, April 27, 1882; ratified by the people, May 22, 1882. Salt Lake City, 1882.
42 p.

Cover title.
Includes journal of proceedings of the constitutional convention.
Admission to statehood, under this constitution, refused by Congress.

[Ut 4]
Utah (Ter.) Constitutional Convention, 1887.
Constitution of the state of Utah and memorial to Congress, asking admission into the Union. [n. p.] 1887.
[2], 27 p.

Cover title.
Admission to statehood, under this constitution, refused by Congress.

[Ut 5]
Utah (Ter.) Constitutional Convention, 1895.
Enabling act, list of officers, members and committees and standing rules of the constitutional convention of Utah. Salt Lake City, March 4, 1895. [Salt Lake City] 1895.
26 p.

Cover title.

[Ut 6]
Utah (Ter.) Constitutional Convention, 1895.
Official report of the proceedings and debates of the convention assembled at Salt Lake City on the fourth day of March, 1895, to adopt a constitution for the state of Utah. Salt Lake City, 1898.
2 v. (2011 p.)

[Ut 7]
Utah (Ter.) Constitutional Convention, 1895.
Constitution of the state of Utah, as framed by the constitutional convention in Salt Lake City, Utah, from March 4 to May 8, 1895 . . . Salt Lake City, 1895.
iii, [1], 48 p.

Cover title.
Published by authority of the convention under the supervision of Hon. Richard G. Lambert, chairman of Committee on Printing.

[Ut 8]
Utah. Constitution.
Constitution of the state of Utah as amended, with annotations. [Sale Lake City] 1941.
1 p. l., 45 p.

[Ut 9]
Utah. Constitution.
Constitution of the state of Utah, as amended, original, and amendments, 1959 . . . Compiled by Utah State Archives. [Salt Lake City, 1959]
viii, 185 p. facsim.

"Facsimile Constitution": p. 55-120.

Vermont

[Vt 1]
Vermont. Constitution.
The constitution of the state of Vermont, as revised by the Council of Censors, and recommended for the consideration of the people. Windsor, 1785.

44 p.

"The Constitution of Vermont, as established by convention in the year 1778": p. 24-44.

[Vt 2]
Vermont. Council of Censors, 1792.
Proceedings of the Council of Censors, of the state of Vermont, at their sessions holden at Rutland, in the year 1792. Published by order of the council, for the inspection of the people, in conformity to the xlth section of the constitution. And for the consideration of the freemen of this state, to convene at Windsor, on the first Wednesday of July 1793. Rutland, 1792.

80 p.

"The Constitution of Vermont, as proposed by the Council of Censors, in the year 1792": p. [7]-36; "The Constitution of Vermont, as established by convention, in the year 1786": p. [47]-80.

[Vt 3]
Vermont. Constitutional Convention, 1793.

Journal of the Vermont constitutional convention held at Windsor July 3, to 9, 1793.

(In Vermont Historical Society. Proceedings for the years 1921-1923. Montpelier, 1924. p. [183]-198)

[Vt 4]
Vermont. Constitution.

The constitution of Vermont, as adopted by the convention, holden at Windsor, July fourth, one thousand seven hundred and ninety-three. Windsor, 1793.

p. [107]-129.

[Vt 5]
Vermont. Council of Censors, 1813-1814.

Journal of the Council of Censors, at their sessions in June and October, 1813, and January, 1814. Middlebury, 1814.

56 p.

[Vt 6]
Vermont. Council of Censors, 1813-1814.

An address of the Council of Censors, to the people of Vermont; together with proposed amendments to the constitution. Montpelier, 1813.

16 p.

[Vt 7]
Vermont. Constitutional Convention, 1814.

Journal of the convention of Vermont, at their session begun and holden at Montpelier . . . on Thursday the seventh day of July A. D. 1814. Published by order of the convention. Danville, 1814.

Convention "assembled . . . for the purpose of taking into consideration certain proposed alterations and amendments to the Constitution of . . . Vermont as agreed upon and recommended by" . . . the Council of Censors.

[Vt 8]
Vermont. Council of Censors, 1820-1821.

Journal of the Council of Censors, at their sessions in June and October, 1820, and March, 1821. Published by order of Council. Danville, 1821.

64 p., fold. table.

[Vt 9]
Vermont. Constitutional Convention, 1822.

Journal of the convention of Vermont, assembled at the State House, at Montpelier, on the 21st day of February, and dissolved on the 23d day of February, 1822. Published by order of the convention. Burlington, 1822.

39 p.

Convention "assembled . . . for the purpose of taking into consideration certain proposed alterations, and amendments to the Constitution of . . . Vermont, as agreed upon and recommended by" . . . the Council of Censors.

Rules of the convention: p. 9-10.

Articles of amendments to the constitution of the state of Vermont, proposed by the Council of Censors on the 24th day of March, A. D. 1821: p. 12-21.

The unanimous address of the Council of Censors, adopted March 26, 1821, to the people of the state of Vermont: p. 22-33.

[Vt 10]
Vermont. Council of Censors, 1827.

Journal of the Council of Censors, at their sessions at Montpelier and Burlington, in June, October, and November, 1827.

48 p.

[Vt 11]
Vermont. Constitutional Convention, 1828.

Journal of the convention of Vermont, convened at the state House at Montpelier, June 26, A. D. 1828. Published by order of the convention. Royalton [1828?]

22 p.

[Vt. 11, cont.]

"Convened . . . for the purpose of taking into consideration certain proposed amendments to the Constitution of . . . Vermont, as agreed upon and recommended by" . . . the Council of Censors.

Articles of amendment to the constitution of the state of Vermont, proposed by the Council of Censors, on the 29th day of November, 1827: p. 10-14.

[Vt 12]
Vermont. Council of Censors, 1834-1835.

Journal of the Council of Censors, at their sessions holden at Montpelier and Middlebury in June and October, 1834, and January, 1835. Published by order of the council. Middlebury, 1835.

68 p.

[Vt 13]
Vermont. Constitutional Convention, 1836.

Journal of the convention holden at Montpelier, on the 6th day of January, A. D. 1836, agreeable to the ordinance of the Council of Censors, made on the 16th day of January, 1835, together with the amendments of the constitution, as adopted by the convention, and the whole of the constitution of the state of Vermont, as now in force. Published by order of the convention. St. Albans, 1836.

124 p.

Articles of amendment, alteration and addition, to the constitution of the state of Vermont, proposed by the Council of Censors on the 15th day of January, A. D. 1835; p. 10-22.

Address "to the people of the State of Vermont": p. 22-35.

Constitution of the state of Vermont [1836] : p. [105]-124.

[Vt 14]
Vermont. Council of Censors, 1841-1842.

Journal of the sessions of the Council of Censors of the state of Vermont, held at Montpelier, in June, and October, A. D. 1841, and at Burlington, in February, A. D. 1842. Burlington, 1842.

75 p.

[Vt 15]
Vermont. Constitutional Convention, 1843.

Journal of the convention, holden at Montpelier, on the fourth day of January, A. D. 1843, agreeable to the ordinance of the Council of Censors, made on the fourteenth day of February, 1842, to consider certain amendments proposed to the constitution of the state of Vermont. Published by order of the convention. Montpelier, 1843.

84 p.

Articles of amendment, and addition to the constitution of the state of Vermont, proposed by the Council of Censors, at their session in February, A. D. 1842: p. 10-17.

Address "To the Freemen of the State of Vermont": p. 17-24.
Rules of the convention: p. 34-36.

[Vt 16]
Vermont. Council of Censors, 1848-1849.

The journal of the Council of Censors of the state of Vermont, at their several sessions in Montpelier and Burlington, 1848-1849. Published by authority. Burlington, 1849.

1 p. l., [5]-87 p.

[Vt 17]
Vermont. Constitutional Convention, 1850.

Journal of the constitutional convention, holden at Montpelier, on the second day of January, A. D. 1850, agreeable to the ordinance of the Council of Censors, made on the twenty-eighth day of February, 1849, to consider certain amendments proposed to the constitution of the state of Vermont. Published by order of the convention. Burlington, 1850.

114 p.

Articles of amendment proposed by the council: p. 21-28.
Address of the council: p. 28-36.
Rules of the convention: p. 41-43.

[Vt 18]
Vermont. Constitution.
The constitution of the state of Vermont, adopted by convention held in the year of our Lord 1777, and amended by conventions held in the years 1786, 1793, 1828, 1836, and 1850. Published by order of the General Assembly. Montpelier, 1852.
56 p.

[Vt 19]
Vermont. Council of Censors, 1855-1856.
The journal of the Council of Censors of the state of Vermont at their several sessions in Montpelier and Middlebury 1855-1856. Published by authority. Middlebury, 1856.
108 p.

[Vt 20]
Vermont. Constitutional Convention, 1857.
Journal of the proceedings of the constitutional convention, assembled at Montpelier, on the first Wednesday of January, 1857. Burlington, 1856 [1857]
39 p.

Rules of the convention: p. 10-12.
Appendix: Articles of amendment proposed by the Council of Censors, February, 1856: p. [33]-39.

[Vt 21]
Vermont. Council of Censors, 1869.
Journal of the Council of Censors of the state of Vermont, at its several sessions held in Montpelier, 1869. Published by order of council. Montpelier, 1869.
106 p., 1 l.

[Vt 22]
Vermont. Council of Censors, 1869.
Minority report of Special Committee on Changing the Mode of Amending the Constitution. Council of Censors—second ses-

[Vt. 22, cont.]
sion, 1869. [Montpelier? 1869?]
    11 p.

    No title page.

[Vt 23]
Vermont. Constitutional Convention, 1870.
    Journal of the proceedings of the constitutional convention of
the people of Vermont, begun and held at the State House in
Montpelier, on the 8th of June, 1870. Printed by authority.
Burlington, 1870.
    75, iii p.
    Articles of amendment to the constitution of the state of Ver-
mont proposed by the Council of Censors on the 22d day of
October, A. D. 1869: p. 17-27.
    Address "To the people of the State of Vermont": p. 28-29.
    Rules of the convention: p. 30-32.

[Vt 24]
Vermont. Constitution.
    The constitution as established July 9, 1793, and amended in
1828, 1836, 1850, 1870, and 1883, including the Declaration of
Independence, the Articles of Confederation, and the Constitution of the United States. Issued by authority. [Montpelier?
1883?]
    [4], 69 p.

[Vt 25]
**Vermont. Commission to Prepare and Present Proposals of Amend-
        ment to the Constitution.**
    Proposals of amendment to constitution; report of commission
appointed under joint resolution approved November 11, 1908.
January 6, 1910. St. Albans, 1910.
    55 p.
    At head of title: State of Vermont.
    Frank C. Partridge, Frank L. Greene, and others, commis-
sioners.

[Vt 26]
Vermont. Constitution.
Constitution of the state of Vermont, established July 9, 1793, and amended in 1828, 1836, 1850, 1870, 1883, and 1913. Published by secretary of state. [Burlington] 1913.
160 p.

[Vt 27]
Vermont. Commission to Prepare and Present Proposals of Amendment to the Constitution.
Proposals of amendment to constitution; report of commission. December 1, 1920. Montpelier, 1920.
22 p.

[Vt 28]
Vermont. Constitution.
Constitution of the state of Vermont, established July 9, 1793, and amended in 1828, 1836, 1850, 1870, 1883, 1913, and 1924. Published by secretary of state. [Montpelier?] 1924.
132 p.

Appendix: governor's proclamation, April 8, 1913, p. 65-68; governor's proclamation, April 8, 1924, p. 68-70.

[Vt 29]
Vermont. Commission on Proposals for Constitutional Amendments.
Report. [Montpelier?] 1931.
12 p.

[Vt 30]
Vermont. Commission on Proposals of Amendments to the Constitution.
Report. [Montpelier?] 1940.
8 p.

[Vt 31]
Vermont. Commission on Proposals of Amendment to the Constitution.
Report. [Montpelier] 1950.
6 p.

[Vt 32]
Vermont. Constitution.
Constitution of the state of Vermont, established July 9, 1793, and amended in 1828, 1836, 1850, 1870, 1883, 1913, 1924, and 1954. [Burlington? 1954?]
134 p.

Virginia

[Va 1]
Virginia (Colony) Convention, May 6, 1776.
The proceedings of the convention of delegates, held at the Capitol, in the city of Williamsburg, in the colony of Virginia, on Monday, the 6th of May, 1776. Williamsburg [1776]
185 p.

"A declaration of rights made by the representatives of the good people of Virginia, assembled in full and free convention": p. 100-103.

[Va 2]
Virginia (Colony) Convention, May 6, 1776.
Ordinances passed at a general convention of delegates and representatives from the several counties and corporations of Virginia, held at the Capitol, in the city of Williamsburg, on Monday the 6th of May, anno Dom. 1776. Williamsburg [1776?]
44 p.

[Va 3]
Virginia. Constitution.
The constitution of Virginia—1776.

(In Thorpe, Francis Newton, comp. The federal and state constitutions, colonial charters, and other organic laws of the states, territories, and colonies now or heretofore forming the United States of America. Washington, 1909. v. 7, p. 3812-3819)

[Va 4]
Virginia. Staunton Convention, 1816.
Journal of the proceedings of a convention, begun and held at
Staunton, the 19th day of August, in the year 1816. [Staunton?
1816]
16 p.

As a result of a mass meeting at Winchester in 1816, calling for
a convention, sixty-nine delegates from thirty-eight western moun-
tain counties met at Staunton and petitioned the General Assembly for a new state constitution which would give them representation in elections proportionate to their population. Cf. F. M.
Green. Constitutional development in the South Atlantic States,
1776-1860. 1930.

[Va 6]
Virginia. Constitutional Convention, 1829-1830.
Journal, acts and proceedings, of a general convention of the
commonwealth of Virginia, assembled in Richmond, on Monday,
the fifth day of October, in the year of our Lord one thousand
eight hundred and twenty-nine. Richmond, 1829.
302, 187, 8 p.

"An amended constitution or form of government for Virginia.
[Adopted January 13, 1830] ": p. 2-8 at end.

[Va 7]
Virginia. Constitutional Convention, 1829-1830.
Proceedings and debates of the Virginia state convention of
1829-1830. To which are subjoined, the new constitution of Virginia, and the votes of the people . . . Richmond, 1830.
iv, 919 p.

[Va 8]
Virginia. Constitutional Convention, 1850-1851.
Journal, acts and proceedings of a general convention of the
state of Virginia, assembled at Richmond, on Monday, the four-

[Va 8, cont.]

teenth day of October, eighteen hundred and fifty. Richmond, 1850.

424, [533] p.

Includes appendix to the journal, being a journalized account of the proceedings of the Committee of the Whole upon the basis of representation, 23 p.—Resolutions, reports of committees, and amendments proposed thereto, and a declaration of rights.

New constitution of the commonwealth of Virginia, adopted by the state convention, sitting in the city of Richmond on the 31st day of July, 1851. Richmond 1851, 36 p., has separate title page.

[Va 9]

Virginia. Constitutional Convention, 1850-1851.

Register of the debates and proceedings of the Virginia Reform Convention. Wm. G. Bishop, official reporter. Richmond, 1851.

1 v. (various pagings)

From supplements to daily papers. No complete set extant.

[Va 10]

Virginia. Auditor's Office.

Documents, containing statistics of Virginia, ordered to be printed by the state convention sitting in the city of Richmond, 1850-1851. Richmond, 1851.

[547] p.

"An act to take the sense of the people upon the call of a convention and providing for organizing the same. Richmond, 1850.": 7 p. at end.

[Va 11]

Virginia. Constitution.

The new constitution of Virginia, with the amended bill of rights, as adopted by the Reform Convention of 1850-1851. Richmond, 1859.

35 p.

[Va 12]
Virginia. Convention, Richmond, 1861.

Journal of the acts and proceedings of a general convention of the state of Virginia, assembled at Richmond, on Wednesday, the thirteenth day of February, eighteen hundred and sixty-one. Richmond, 1861.

1 v. (various pagings)

This volume also includes appendix to the journal, portions of the journal of the secret session, ordinances adopted, reports from the Committee on Federal Relations, Virginia bill of rights, and the new constitution adopted in 1861.

[Va 13]
Virginia. Convention, Richmond, 1861.

[Documents of the convention 1-54. Richmond? 1861]
1 v. (various pagings)

[Va 15]
Virginia. Constitutional Convention, Alexandria, 1864.

Journal of the constitutional convention, which convened at Alexandria on the 13th day of February, 1864. Alexandria, 1864.
52 p.

The convention, which met at Alexandria February 13 to April 11, 1864, consisted of seventeen delegates from such portions of Virginia as were then within the Union lines and had not been included in the recently formed state of West Virginia.

[Va 16]
Virginia. Constitutional Convention, Alexandria, 1864.

[Documents. Alexandria, 1864]
1 v. (various pagings)

[Va 17]
Virginia. Constitution.

Constitution of Virginia—1864. [Plus amendment ratified in 1865]

[Va 17, cont.]

(In Thorpe, Francis Newton, comp. The federal and state constitutions, colonial charters, and other organic laws of the states, territories, and colonies now or heretofore forming the United States of America. Washington, 1909. v. 7, p. 3852-3871)

[Va 18]
Virginia. Constitutional Convention, 1867-1868.
Journal of the constitutional convention of the state of Virginia, convened in the city of Richmond December 3, 1867, by an order of General Schofield, dated November 2, 1867, in pursuance of the act of Congress of March 23, 1867. Richmond, 1867 [1868]
391 p.

[Va 19]
Virginia. Constitutional Convention, 1867-1868.
The debates and proceedings of the constitutional convention of the state of Virginia, assembled at the city of Richmond, Tuesday, December 3, 1867: being a full and complete report of the debates and proceedings of the convention, together with the reconstruction acts of Congress and those supplementary thereto, the order of the commander of the First Military District assembling the convention, and the new constitution. Official: W. H. Samuel, phonographic reporter. Richmond, 1868.
750 p.

[Va 20]
Virginia. Constitutional Convention, 1867-1868.
Documents of the constitutional convention of the state of Virginia. Richmond, 1867 [1868]
310 p., folded chart.

[Va 21]
Address of the conservative members of the late state convention to the people of Virginia. [Richmond, 1868]
8 p.

Caption title.

[Va 22]
Virginia. Constitution.
Amendments to the constitution of 1870 [ratified 1872, 1874, 1876, and 1882]

(In Thorpe, Francis Newton, comp. The federal and state constitutions, colonial charters, and other organic laws of the states, territories, and colonies now or heretofore forming the United States of America. Washington, 1909. v. 7, p. 3900-3904)

[Va 23]
Virginia. Constitution.
The constitution of Virginia, an annotated ed., by Armistead R. Long . . . Together with a reprint of the previous constitutions of Virginia. Lynchburg, 1901.
xvi, 194 p.

[Va 24]
Virginia. Constitutional Convention, 1901-1902.
Journal of the constitutional convention of Virginia. Held in the city of Richmond, beginning June 12, 1901. Richmond, 1901[1902]
1 v. (various pagings)

Contains many documents and committee reports and "The Constitution of the State of Virginia, adopted by the Convention of 1901-1902. Published by authority. Richmond, 1902."

[Va 25]
Virginia. Constitutional Convention, 1901-1902.
Report of the proceedings and debates of the constitutional convention, state of Virginia. Held in the city of Richmond June 12, 1901, to June 26, 1902 . . . Richmond, 1906.
2 v. (3297 p.)
J. H. Lindsay, editor and compiler.

[Va 26]
Virginia. Constitutional Convention, 1901-1902.
Virginia constitutional convention directory, 1901. Richmond [1901?]
93 p.

[Va 27]
Virginia. Constitutional Convention, 1901-1902.
  Manual. Richmond, 1901.
  82 p., plate.

[Va 28]
Virginia. Constitution.
  An annotated constitution of Virginia: exhibiting under one
view and at a glance . . . both the old and new constitutions, and
the changes made by the new; and annotated with all the Virginia
decisions construing the old provisions of the new constitution,
and with important decisions of sister states and the Supreme
Court of the United States touching the new provisions; with an
appendix giving ordinances for the registration of voters and the
extension of charters, and the statutes authorizing the constitution. By Sam N. Hurst . . . Luray, 1903.
  xviii, 241 [i. e., 242] p.

[Va 29]
Virginia. Constitution.
  Constitution of Virginia . . . Richmond, 1923.
  172 p.

  Includes amendments ratified at the general election of November 8, 1920.

[Va 30]
Virginia. Commission to Suggest Amendments to the Constitution.
  The constitution of Virginia. Report of the Commission to Sug-
gest Amendments to the Constitution to the General Assembly of
Virginia. To be submitted to the extra session March, 1927.
Richmond, 1927.
  xii, 82 p. (Virginia. General Assembly, 1927 House Doc. 2)

[Va 31]
Virginia. Secretary of the Commonwealth.
  Statement of vote for and against certain proposed amend-

[Va 31, cont.]
ments to the constitution of Virginia, cast in the general election
held the first Thursday after the first Monday in November, 1927.

(In his Report . . . for the year ending June 30, 1928. p. 377-
384)

[Va 32]
Virginia. Governor, 1926-1930 (Harry F. Byrd)
The constitution of Virginia. A discussion of the amendments
proposed to the constitution of Virginia. Election, June 19, 1928.
[Richmond, 1928]
24 p.

[Va 33]
Virginia. Constitution.
Proposed amendments to the constitution of Virginia. Agreed
to by the General Assembly of Virginia at the regular session of
1926 and the extra session of 1927, approved by the General Assembly at the regular session of 1928. Submitted by an act approved March 14, 1928, for ratification or rejection by the
people of Virginia at a special election to be held on June 19,
1928. [Richmond, 1928]
71 p.

[Va 34]
Virginia. Laws, statutes, etc.
Chapter 1, An act to provide for submitting to the qualified
voters of Virginia the question whether there shall be a convention to revise and amend certain provisions of the constitution
of Virginia [relating to payment of poll taxes by members of the
armed forces] and providing an appropriation therefor. Approved
December 16, 1944. [Richmond, 1945]
6 p.

Caption title.
At head of title: Acts of the General Assembly, extra session,
1944/1945.

[Va 35]
Virginia. Constitutional Convention, 1945.

Journal of the constitutional convention of the commonwealth of Virginia to amend the constitution of Virginia for voting by certain members of the armed forces. Held in the Old Hall
of the House of Delegates in the State Capitol at Richmond
April 30, May 1, 2, 22, 1945 [and] appendix. Richmond, 1945.
    235 p.

Compiled by the secretary of the convention, E. Griffith
Dodson.

[Va 36]
Dodson, Edward Griffith, comp.

Information concerning constitutional convention, commencing
April 30, 1945. Limited edition for members of the convention.
Compiled by E. Griffith Dodson, clerk of the House of Delegates.
[Richmond, 1945]
    [110] p. incl. tabl., forms.

Contents.—Governor's proclamation for special session—Governor's message, special session 1944.—Act for election on question
of convention.—Supreme Court of Appeals' opinion on constitu-
tionality of act for special session. Statement of votes cast in election.—Governor's proclamation for special session.—Governor's
message, special session 1945.—Act for convention and election
of delegates.—War voters act.—Act for national elections, chapter 286.—Act for payment of poll taxes, chapter 287.—Act for
state elections, chapter 288.—Districts, members of the convention and post offices.—Members of the convention and districts
represented.—Biographical sketches.

[Va 37]
Virginia. Constitution.

Constitution of Virginia, as amended June 19, 1928, November
7, 1944, May 3, 1945, November 5, 1946, November 2, 1948,
November 7, 1950, and November 4, 1952. Richmond, 1953.
    114 p.

[Va 38]
Virginia. Constitutional Convention, 1956.

Journal of the constitutional convention of the commonwealth of Virginia to revise and amend sec. 141 of the constitution of Virginia held in the Old Hall of the House of Delegates in the State Capitol at Richmond, March 5, 6, 7, 1956. And appendix. [Compiled by E. Griffith Dodson, secretary of the convention] Richmond, 1956.

116, [103] p., plate.

Appendix includes Report of Commission on Public Education (Gray report), interposition resolution, decisions of U. S. Supreme Court of May 17, 1954 and May 31, 1955, and other documents.

[Va 39]
Virginia. Constitution.

Constitution of Virginia. As amended June 19, 1928, November 7, 1944, May 3, 1945, November 5, 1946, November 2, 1948, November 7, 1950, November 4, 1952, March 7, 1956, and November 6, 1956. Richmond, 1956.

114 p.

Washington

[Wa 1]
Washington (Ter.) Constitutional Convention, 1878.
 Washington's first constitution, 1878, and proceedings of the convention, edited by Edmond S. Meany . . . [and] John T. Condon . . . [Seattle? 1919?]
 104 p.

 Reprinted from the Washington Historical Quarterly, 1918-1919.

[Wa 2]
Washington (Ter.) Constitutional Convention, 1889.
 The journal of the Washington State constitutional convention, 1889, with analytical index by Quentin Shipley Smith. Edited by Beverly Paulik Rosenow. Seattle [1962]
 xv, 931 p.

 Bibliography: p. 931.

[Wa 3]
Washington. Constitution.
 . . . Constitution of the state of Washington, proposed by the convention, held at Olympia, commencing July 4, 1889, and ending August 22, 1889. Olympia, 1889.
 1 p. l., 28 p.

[Wa 3, cont.]
At head of title: published by authority.
Proclamation of the governor, April 15th, 1889, authorizing
the election of delegates to the constitutional convention, and
proclamation, August 27, 1889, authorizing a general election for
the ratification or rejection of the constitution: 2 fold. leaves inserted at end of volume.

[Wa 4]
Washington. Constitution.
Constitution of the state of Washington, with marginal notes
and full index, prepared by Andrew Woods . . . Seattle, 1889.
74 p.

[Wa 5]
Washington. Constitution.
. . . Enabling act and state constitution, with side notes and
index. Published by authority of the superintendent of public
instruction. Olympia, 1905.
88 p.

[Wa 6]
Washington. Advisory Constitutional Revision Commission.
Report. Olympia, 1935.
40, [1] p.

[Wa 7]
Washington. Constitution.
Constitution of the state of Washington annotated. Adopted
August 22, 1889, with amendments up to and including those
adopted at the state general election, November 4, 1952. Annotated and indexed by the publisher's editorial staff. San Francisco, 1953.
lxv, 595 p.

The Constitution of the United States: p. ix-xxxiv.

[Wa 8]
Washington. Constitution.

Constitution of the United States and the state of Washington. 1961-1962 ed. Olympia, 1961.

226 p.

West Virginia

[WV 1]
Lewis, Virgil Anson, ed.

How West Virginia was made. Proceedings of the first convention of the people of northwestern Virginia at Wheeling, May 13, 14, and 15, 1861, and the journal of the second convention of the people of northwestern Virginia at Wheeling, which assembled, June 11, 1861, and continued in session until June 25. Adjourned until August 6, 1861. Reassembled on that date, and continued in session until August 21, when it adjourned sine die. With appendixes and an introduction, annotations and addenda . . . [Charleston] 1909.

337, xii p., front.

Records transcribed from the Daily Intelligencer of Wheeling.

Publication directed by Hon. William G. Conley, attorney general of West Virginia, December 1, 1909.

"Events occurring in the history of West Virginia. From the adjournment of the second convention of the people of northwestern Virginia, August 21, 1861, to the admission of the State into the Union, June 20, 1863": p. [317]-337.

[WV 2]
Virginia. Convention, Wheeling, 1861-1863.

Journal of the constitutional convention of West Virginia, assembled at Wheeling on Tuesday, November the twenty-sixth, eighteen hundred and sixty-one [With appendix] Wheeling, 1861.

1 v. (various pagings)

[WV 3]
Virginia. Convention, Wheeling, 1861-1863.
Debates and proceedings of the first constitutional convention of West Virginia (1861-1863). Edited by Charles H. Ambler, Frances Haney Atwood, and William B. Mathews, under the direction of the Supreme Court of Appeals of West Virginia. Huntington [1939?]
3 v.

V. II-III have caption title only.

[WV 4]
Virginia. Convention, Wheeling, 1861-1863.
Ordinances of the convention assembled at Wheeling, on the 11th of June, 1861. Printed by authority of the convention. Wheeling, 1861.
p. [39]-62.

[WV 5]
Virginia. Convention, Wheeling, 1861-1863.
Address of the delegates composing the new state constitutional convention to their constituents. Edited by C. H. Ambler.

(Reprinted in West Virginia. Dept. of Archives and History. West Virginia history . . . 1941-1942. v. 3, p. 156-170)

[WV 6]
Virginia. Convention, Wheeling, 1861-1863.
. . . Memorial of the commission appointed by the convention of West Virginia [November, 1861] praying for the admission of that state into the Union. [Washington, 1862]
13 p. ([U. S.] 37th Cong., 2d sess. Senate. Misc. Doc. 99)

Caption title.
May 31, 1862. Referred to the Committee on Territories and orders to be printed.

[WV 7]
West Virginia. Constitution.
Amended constitution of West Virginia, adopted by the convention February 18, 1863. [n. p., 1863?]
    32 p.

    Caption title.

[WV 8]
West Virginia. Constitutional Convention, 1872.
Journal of constitutional convention, assembled at Charleston, West Virginia, January 16, 1872 . . . Charleston, 1872.
    353 p.

    p. 17 incorrectly numbered 71; p. 292 incorrectly numbered 262.

[WV 9]
West Virginia. Constitutional Convention, 1872.
Standing committees and rules of the constitutional convention, Charleston, 1872.
    1 v. (various pagings)

    Includes census, various plans for the judiciary, and reports of committees.

[WV 10]
West Virginia. Constitution.
Constitution and schedule, adopted in convention at Charleston, April 9, 1872 . . . Charleston, 1872.
    47 p.

[WV 11]
West Virginia. Reasons why the new constitution should not be adopted. [n. p., 1872?]
    8 p.

    Caption title.

[WV 12]
West Virginia. Constitution.
Constitution of West Virginia, annotated from decisions of supreme courts of West Virginia, Virginia, and United States. Edited by W. M. Justis, Jr. . . . Richmond, 1905.
183, vi p.

Accompanied by loose sheets containing additions to "Annotations to code of West Virginia. Edited by W. M. Justis, Jr."

[WV 13]
West Virginia. Commission to Study the Constitution.
The constitution of West Virginia; report of commission appointed pursuant to House joint resolution no. 5 adopted by the legislature of the state of West Virginia, March, 9, 1929, to study the constitution and to submit amendments thereto . . . [Charleston? 1930?]
xii, 49 p.

Filed with the governor of West Virginia, December 1, 1930.

[WV 14]
West Virginia. Constitution.
The constitution of West Virginia, ratified in 1872 . . . Charleston, 1950.
44 p., 1 l.

Wisconsin

[Wi 1]
Wisconsin. Constitutional Convention, 1846.
Journal of the convention to form a constitution for the state of Wisconsin: begun and held at Madison, on the fifth day of October, one thousand, eight hundred and forty-six. Madison, 1847.
506 p.

The constitution framed by this convention was submitted to popular vote in April, 1847, and was rejected by the people.

[Wi 2]
Quaife, Milo Milton, ed.
The convention of 1846. Madison, 1919.
827 p., plates, ports., facsim. (Publications of the State Historical Society of Wisconsin. Collections, v. XXVII. Constitutional series, v. II)

The constitution of 1846: p. 732-755.

[Wi 3]
Wisconsin. Constitutional Convention, 1847-1848.
Journal of the convention to form a constitution for the state of Wisconsin, with a sketch of the debates, begun and held at Madison, on the fifteenth day of December, eighteen hundred and forty-seven. By authority of the convention. Madison, 1848.
1 p. l., 678 p., fold. plan, fold. table.

[Wi 3, cont.]

The convention adjourned February 1, 1848. The constitution framed by this convention was submitted to the people and accepted by them in March, 1848.

"Constitution of the State of Wisconsin. Adopted in convention at Madison, February 1, A. D. 1848": p. [601]-627.

"Constitution of the State of Wisconsin. Adopted in convention at Madison, December 16, A. D. 1846": p. [628]-652.

[Wi 4]
Quaife, Milo Milton, ed.

The attainment of statehood. [Madison, c1928]

xiii p., 1 l., 965 p. (Publications of the State Historical Society of Wisconsin. Collections, v. XXIX. Constitutional series, v. IV)

"Journal and debates of Constitutional Convention of 1847-1848" (p. [175]-883) supplemented by such additional information gathered from the press and elsewhere, as has been available. Cf. Pref.

[Wi 5]
Wisconsin. Constitution.

Constitutions of the United States and of the state of Wisconsin, with amendments and history up to 1935; also a brief history of the admission of Wisconsin to the Union, and of the organic law of Wisconsin from 1787 to 1848. Published by authority of Bureau of Purchases. Madison, 1935.

1 p. l., p. 11-48.

Constitution of the United States: p. 13-23.

"Historical outline of the admission of Wisconsin to the Union. By Reuben G. Thwaites, secretary and superintendent of the State Historical Society of Wisconsin": p. 46-48.

[Wi 6]
Wisconsin. Constitution.

The Wisconsin constitution, 1963. [Madison, 1965]

31 p.

Reprinted from 1964 Wisconsin Blue Book.

Wyoming

[Wy 1]
Wyoming (Ter.) Governor.

Proclamation [issued June 3, 1889, directing an election on the second Monday in July, of delegates to a constitutional convention at Cheyenne, to be held the first Monday in September, 1889. Cheyenne, 1889]

[3] p.

[Wy 2]
Wyoming (Ter.) Constitutional Convention, 1889.

Journal and debates of the constitutional convention of the state of Wyoming, begun at the city of Cheyenne on September 2, 1889, and concluded September 30, 1889.

864, 60, 15, [1] p.

"Constitution": 60 p., following p. 864.

[Wy 3]
Wyoming (Ter.) Constitutional Convention, 1889.

Memorial to the President and Congress for the admission of Wyoming Territory to the Union. With appendices, showing the action taken by the people, and the constitution, as adopted. Cheyenne, 1889.

xiv, p., 1 l., 75, [1] p.

Signed by Memorial Committee appointed by constitutional convention.

[Wy 4]
Wyoming. Constitution.

Constitution of the state of Wyoming, including all amendments adopted to May 1, 1959. [Cheyenne? 1959?]

48 p., illus.